The After-Dinner Gardening Book

The After-Dinner Gardening Book

by Richard W. Langer

Illustrations by Susan McNeill

Ten Speed Press
Berkeley, California

1☯

TEN SPEED PRESS
P.O. Box 7123
Berkeley, California 94707

FIRST TEN SPEED PRINTING 1992

Cover design by Nancy Austin
Text design by Les Ferriss
Typesetting by Wilsted & Taylor
Illustrations by Susan McNeill

Library of Congress Cataloging-in-Publication Data

Langer, Richard W.
The after-dinner gardening book / Richard W. Langer ;
illustrations by Susan McNeill.
p.   cm.
Includes bibliographical references.
ISBN 0-89815-450-2
1. Indoor gardening.   2. Plant propagation.   3. Fruit-culture.
I. Title.
SB419.L348   1992
635.9′86—dc20   91-33255
CIP

Printed in the United States of America

1   2   3   4   5   -   96   95   94   93   92

Contents

Acknowledgments

First and foremost, I wish to thank my wife, Susan, who not only supplied the illustrations and typed numerous drafts of the manuscript, but adjusted happily to living in a jungle. Also, my warm appreciation to Mrs. Sonia Wedge, Mrs. Lothian Lynas, and Mr. John F. Reed, whose invaluable help, patience, and knowledge guided my research in their wonderfully complete New York Botanical Gardens Library. My special thanks to Dr. Malcolm C. Shurtleff, Professor of Plant Pathology and Extension Specialist at the University of Illinois, and Dr. Ivan Buddenhagen, Professor and Chairman of the Department of Plant Pathology at the University of Hawaii, for their kind diagnostic assistance in dealing with problem plants.

Introduction

The conversion of our apartment from a normal, barren city cave to a tropical jungle began quite by accident one bleak winter day. I was sitting huddled in pajamas and two dressing gowns, a wool scarf around my throat, tending a particularly tenacious New York cold. My wife, Susan, in complete innocence, had left beside me a large warm glass of freshly squeezed lemonade with honey and set off to the local pharmacy for aspirin. I myself sat unsuspecting, halfheartedly reading a spy novel. Dutifully I took a slug of the lemonade, almost choking on two seeds which had slipped seditiously into the brew. That, I think, was the exact moment it all began.

There was no saucer, and to put the seeds back in the lemonade would only be to court further disaster. Of course I could have gotten up and disposed of them in the kitchen, but such exertion seemed uncalled-for. With only a moment's hesitation I reached over to the bedraggled begonia on the windowsill, abandoned by the previous tenant, and put the pits in the pot. After all, I told myself, they're organic, maybe as they rot they'll fertilize the poor begonia—in its condition nothing could hurt. Then I dozed off until Susan returned, totally unaware of what fruit my innocent act would bear. . . .

A few weeks later, my eye happened to rest on the lone flowerpot and observed a new sprout. Excitedly I called Susan over, congratulating her on rescuing the begonia from the elements of destruction, New York soot being not the least of these. She looked for a moment, then told me:

"It's been invaded. My flowerpot's been invaded."

"Nonsense," I replied.

Thereupon she pointed out what I, even without any botanical training whatsoever, should have noticed. Whereas the begonia leaves were somewhat wrinkled and roundish, the new leaves were long, flat, and shiny. Suddenly, from the dregs of memory, floated up a page out of my Biology 101 textbook: seed leaves. With elaborate erudition I explained how seed leaves, the first two leaves on a new plant, never look like the rest. I couldn't explain why, being unable to recall the next page in the text, but for a while anyhow her invasion theory was eliminated.

The next two leaves appeared ten days later. They were long, flat, and shiny. Slightly shamefaced, I mumbled something about going out for some pipe tobacco, but made my way instead to the local flower shop. As I stood in front of the florist's window debating how to present my problem to him, the obvious answer appeared behind my reflection—in the form of a lemon tree bearing a $9.95 label. I had grown my own tree from seed!

Proud as a new father, I paced up and down before the shop window, letting the tree grow in my imagination until it well shaded the beach bungalow on the tropical island to which I had transported us. Reluctantly giving up the idea of getting cigars to pass around to friends, I headed for a discount store. There I purchased the largest pot they had and several pounds of sterilized soil—newborn plants must be sensitive and all that.

Digging out the lemon tree with Susan's nail file, my first miniature gardening tool, I transplanted it to its new home. When I called Susan over to inspect my handiwork, I was rewarded by a fit of giggles. Well, granted, the pot, about twenty

2

times the size of the plant, did look somewhat underfilled, still . . .

Continuing to sulk at dinnertime, I ate in silence, oblivious to everything except the thought that when "the old cold," as Susan dubbed the lemon tree, started bearing fruit, I'd have the last laugh.

We had fresh mango for dessert. After one bite I stopped suddenly.

"A pit."

"Impossible. How could I miss something that size?"

"No, no. I mean, where is it?"

"I threw them out."

It was one of those moments I was glad ours was an older apartment, without a convenient incinerator chute. I dashed to the kitchen, where I rooted around in the garbage like a pig for truffles, rising at last triumphantly with two beautiful mango pits.

Excusing myself hastily, I ran down to the discount store again, bought two more pots and three huge bags of soil, and returned to Susan's despairing "Oh no!" Then I began my new career as New York's only plantation manager in earnest.

I

A Down-to-Earth Beginning: Including Visits to the Park and Local Construction Sites

Inhabiting this immense globe we call earth—made as it is in large measure of good old-fashioned dirt—I assumed the last problem I would face as an aspiring horticulturist would be a lack of soil. City gardeners, however, as I discovered, are not as fortunate as their suburban counterparts, who can step out their own doors to choose at random from among several square feet of backyard the potting soil they might need. Somewhere beneath the thirty-odd feet of concrete, subway tunnels, storm sewers, and the like that make up the "ground" in the city, there may still exist honest-to-goodness soil, capable of supporting life. Whatever the case, it's unreachable.

Thus I set off one Saturday afternoon with a bucket and a soup spoon, the closest thing to a shovel I could find in our apartment, in search of some potting soil. The local open patch of land called a park seemed the most likely prospect. Upon arrival I selected a not too conspicuous spot behind some trampled bushes and set to work.

My initial elation at finding what looked like really rich black soil evaporated as I scraped away what turned out to be a layer of soot. Followed by a layer of gum wrappers, then another of Popsicle sticks. At last I reached terra firma, and it was firma all right, like blacktop almost. Though it seemed most unpromising, I decided that, having gone this far, I might as well take some home. If nothing else, it should support cacti. Chiseling chunks loose with the spoon, I began piling them into the bucket.

So intent was I upon my task, I didn't notice anyone approaching until a pair of black shoes had planted themselves firmly in front of my bucket. Looking up slowly along the pants, past the gun belt and the badge, I smiled and said:

"Good morning, Officer."

He tapped the bucket with his night stick in reply.

"The sandbox is down by the swings."

Rising slowly on stiff knees, I explained that I needed some potting soil for the pineapples I hoped to plant that afternoon. The expression on his face clearly indicated I wasn't making too good a case for myself. Hastily I added that I grew plants on my windowsill, as a sort of hobby.

He remained dubious, but shifted his questioning to the contents of my apartment. Had I previously taken soil from the park? he wanted to know. No, I explained, I had used a potting soil from the discount store before. That appeared to satisfy him. But, I continued, there really didn't seem much use in buying soil when there was a whole parkful just two blocks from the apartment.

I won't go into the lengthy lecture on defacing city property, depriving the state of revenue, and other fine legal points, to which I then listened attentively. Suffice it to say I left the park under the watchful eye of the police officer, my bucket filled only with a rattling spoon.

The packaged potting soil available at the supermarket or discount store is better anyhow, I soon learned. It is usually sterilized, lessening the chance of fungi and other diseases developing on the plants. Also it is free of stray seeds or roots that might sprout and confuse the issue. When I began my planting, I had only a vague idea of what the plants would look like,

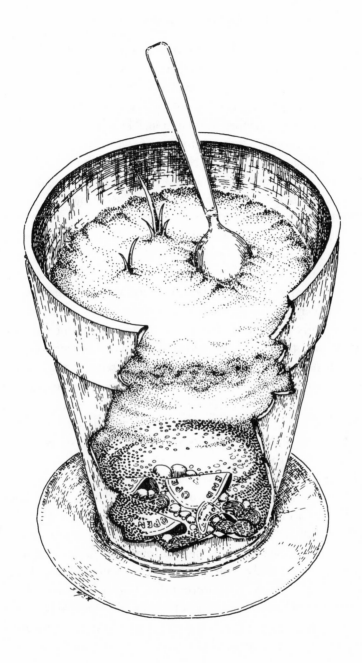

and most likely couldn't have told the difference between a young maple and a papaya. In fact . . . but later for that story.

Once having decided to become an indoor gardener in earnest, I began picking up not only potting soil, but humus as well. The latter enriches the soil; it also keeps it from packing. Potted plants need a lighter mixture of soil than those in a garden. There are no worms or burrowing insects to turn the soil in a pot; as a result a very heavy mixture tends to cake and harden, destroying the hair roots and stunting the plant's growth or even slowly killing it.

Vermiculite, which can also be bought at the gardening counters of some supermarkets and discount stores as well as at gardening centers, is excellent for keeping soil from packing. It has no nutritional value, however, and should be used sparingly, never as a substitute for humus.

Generally I use about two parts potting soil to one part humus in my pots, with an additional handful of vermiculite. Some firms sell a prepackaged mix of the three, but purchasing them separately has advantages. You can make up an extra-rich mixture for certain plants, such as bananas, for which I've had best results with about one-fourth soil and three-fourths humus. Other plants, prickly pears, for instance, seem to like sand added to their soil.

For most jungle crops, sand in the potting mixture itself is not an important factor. However, I've found it a good practice to put half an inch or so of the large-grained, gravelly variety at the bottom of all my pots, for good drainage. To ensure that the loose sand will not run right through the drainage hole, I cover it with slightly bent lids from frozen orange juice cans. The tops must be bent to prevent their packing down over the hole completely, sealing it off. This layering regulates the flow of water through the pot, keeping the soil moist, yet properly drained. The sand should be quite rough. Fine sand will pack, producing the opposite of the desired effect by retaining the water, which then stagnates. One of the principal bugaboos of healthy potted plants is souring of the soil due to standing water, with consequent rotting of the plant's roots in the bog.

Fish tank gravel, which is coarse and quite good for lining the bottom of pots, can be found in any pet store. But I was at a loss for a place to find fine sand for my soil mixture, particularly for a pot I had reserved for prickly pears. In most cases an overly rich soil will not harm a plant, but since the prickly pear is a cactus I felt a sandy mixture was definitely called for. About the only place I could think of for getting sand was the seashore. And not only was it the middle of winter at the time, but I wasn't even sure I could completely remove the salt—an element desirable only at the dinner-table end of gardening.

My problem was solved quite simply one day. Passing a rapidly rising high rise on the way home, I noticed a large pile of sand next to a stack of facing bricks. Having by now learned my lesson, I asked the foreman if I could have a bit for an experiment, carefully avoiding any mention of my plants. Somewhat surprised, he told me to help myself. Collecting from home what I hoped was an inconspicuous shoe box lined with aluminum foil, I returned for my bounty. Barring a few comments from the construction crew about my sandbox, all went well.

Having now found a convenient source for each of the components of my potting mixture—soil, humus, vermiculite, and sand—I was ready for some containers to put them in. Rummaging through the kitchen shelves, I found an amazing variety of potential plant pots. Professional gardeners might not approve of them, but not only can they be made quite attractive, I found they work just fine.

2

Have Some More Coffee, I Need the Can: Or, Pots Homemade and Otherwise

The best container for potted plants is the old standard red clay pot. Its tapered design permits good drainage, and the porous surface leaves the soil well aerated. But it's by no means the only possible pot.

Early in the game I spotted, lined up like tin soldiers against the wall at the back of a kitchen shelf, the empty coffee cans we were saving for cookie overflows. With a screwdriver I punched three small drainage holes in the bottom of each. I briefly considered painting them with the flat latex-based paint left over from decorating our apartment, but rejected that medium as showing dirt much too readily. Instead I settled on a coat of enamel—in subdued colors, so my pots wouldn't outshine the plants themselves—applied carefully to keep any paint, which is toxic, from tainting the inside surfaces.

Besides being inexpensive, these adopted pots have an added advantage when the plants are ready for transplanting to larger containers. All you have to do is lay a canned plant carefully on its side and remove the rusted bottom with a can opener. This requires only a slight struggle. After loosening the soil from the sides with a knife, it is a simple matter to push soil and roots out in one lump ready for repotting.

Milk cartons cut down to about a third their height make excellent starting boxes, again so long as good drainage holes

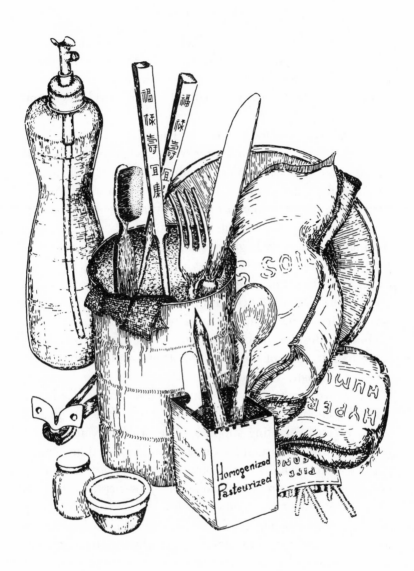

are provided. They have the twin advantages of being always available and disposable. When a seedling is ready for transplanting, the sides of the milk carton are merely cut away with scissors or knife, leaving the seedling undisturbed in its clump of soil.

It was while visiting country cousins, however, that I discovered, at their local gardening center, what must surely be the ultimate in starting pots. Coming in all sizes and shapes, they are molded of compressed fiber and peat. Once seedlings have sprouted and grown to a height three or four times the diameter of the pot—this rule of thumb is easily observable, as the plant will simply begin to look too big for its pot—transplanting is only a matter of burying the entire container in a larger one, always making sure to keep the soil levels the same. After some time the fiber pot dissolves, leaving a rich loamy soil additive. *Voilà!* Instant transplants with no muss, no fuss, no bother. Besides, much to Susan's relief, this method didn't leave half an inch of mud at the bottom of the kitchen sink, where I normally worked.

There were other ways in which I could still wreak havoc with the kitchen, of course. It remained in fact my general store for most planting supplies. The previously mentioned juice-can lids, for instance. Not only are they ideal for screening the drainage holes in the bottom of a pot, but, since they rust, they tend to replenish some of the minerals in the soil used up by a plant as it grows. The little lids are excellent stoppers, even without a layer of gravel over them if the latter is not available, to help stem the flow of water through the pot to the dish beneath.

That dish beneath is something not to be forgotten. There are to this day three perfectly circular watermarks on my desk top from the two mangoes and the pineapple I started after the lemon tree. Discarded aluminum pie pans, of the standard kitchen or the frozen store-bought variety, serve well as saucers for larger pots.

A knife from the table setting early became an indispensable all-around tool for repotting, trimming dead leaves, and pruning, though for the latter task scissors are sometimes better. And any old fork, I soon found, except maybe the dessert kind, will make an excellent miniature pitchfork and rake for turning and loosening soil that has settled, or for burying plant "vitamin pills."

My raids on the kitchen, while not unnoticed, were less disastrous than some of my forays further afield for gardening supplies. When one day, having not even finished Susan's extra-rich homemade pecan pie, I brought home from the supermarket a frozen cheesecake, I thought I was about to bring down a shower of insulted tears. Even after my explanation that I had bought it only for the large deep aluminum pan in which it came, she did not appear fully convinced. During the course of the day, therefore, I ate the entire cheesecake, followed by the pecan pie, before filling the dish with even rows of papaya, pomegranate, and banana seeds. Covering the dish with Saran Wrap, I completed my first miniature greenhouse, retiring to bed with a contented smile and an extreme case of indigestion. After that I more or less refrained from any attempt to conform the family menu to my horticultural requirements, for the most part contenting myself with supplying an occasional dietary supplement of newly discovered tropical fruit.

My first greenhouse was soon superseded by a vastly improved version: I had discovered the existence of cake pans with clear plastic snap-on covers. A large loaf pan makes an ideal miniature hothouse for germinating a good selection of seeds, particularly the smaller variety, such as pomegranate, grape, and papaya.

The first thing to do, I learned the hard way, is to make certain the pan is made of aluminum. I started with one that looked like aluminum, but turned out to be tin-clad steel. It began to rust within a few days, not only making a mess, but also, through "rotting" of the water, killing all the seedlings. Glass or Pyrex, I reflected, would be ideal except for the fact that, being transparent, they let in too much light, and the opaque kind came only in small sizes at the local hardware store. I reverted to aluminum.

Covering the bottom of the pan with four or five single layers of cheesecloth, I added tepid water until the cloth was thoroughly moist, and drained off the excess. I laid out the seeds in even rows, carefully leaving room between different species so that no confusion would occur after growth, hopefully, began. To be doubly certain, on the cover I Scotch-taped labels indicating what types of plants were to sprout beneath, and the date they were planted.

The clear plastic top of this type of pan allows easy seed-watching, at the same time keeping the water from evaporating by letting the condensation drop back into the tin. However, the plastic should be covered with a sheet of paper to darken the interior of the pan, since most seeds germinate best in semidarkness.

The cover itself should not be removed until the seedlings are ready for transplanting. Sealing off the seeds in a miniature greenhouse considerably lessens the ever-present risk of mold attacking the seeds. However, if a serious mold growth develops, it's best to simply dispose of the whole greenhouse, lock, stock, and barrel, as the thousands of mold spores liberated from even a small growth are almost impossible to combat.

Later I began making individual little hothouses out of emptied condiment containers from Chinese takeouts and fast-food chains. I lined them with moist cheesecloth, just like their bigger counterparts, but I kept a separate container for each type

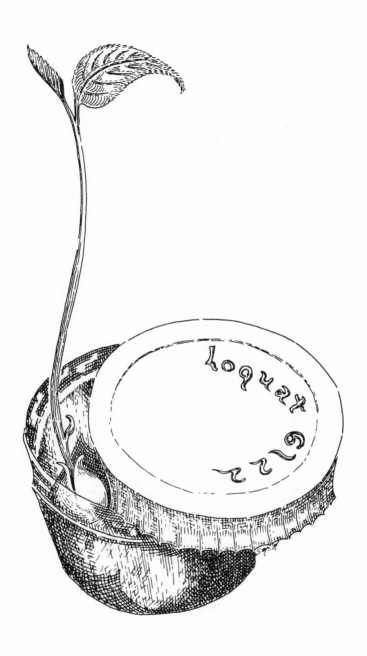

of seed. This eliminated any chance of confusion that might arise when there were several similar seeds sprouting under the same lid. The one thing to remember is to check the seeds with fair regularity. I once forgot about a germinating loquat until it forced the lid off the container by itself. At that point its roots were so tangled in the cheesecloth I had to plant the whole thing, cheesecloth and all. That particular loquat always remained stunted. I don't think it ever got over the Herculean effort of sprouting its way out from under a plastic rock.

In their enclosed environment, without soil, germinating seeds draw nourishment from within until the taproot, the first main root, emerges from the splitting seed, followed by the first leaves. Once the taproot has developed and the seed leaves begin to sprout up, a seedling may be transferred to a pot of its own. I usually have ready for it one of my smaller homemade ones, and bury it gently in a hole poked deep enough to accommodate the root without crowding and to leave the incipient seed leaves just even with the soil line. A transplanted seedling needs profuse watering at once, so the soil will settle evenly around the root before it has a chance to dry out.

As a plant continues to grow, eventually it has to be transferred again. When a plant begins to look too big for its first, homemade pot, I transplant it to a large-sized commercial one, where it can feel comfortably at home for a year or more.

Most of my plants take up their permanent residence in the standard red terra-cotta pots. I don't use their painted counterparts, because enamel eliminates the porous quality of the terra cotta, which is the advantage of commercial containers in the first place—an additional one being, of course, that one doesn't have to eat the desserts they came with.

Even the largest clay pot, however, was at last unable to support Arthur, my first avocado tree, which shot up to well over seven feet and spread out almost five. For him I found an attractive redwood tub held together with brass hoops. The one problem this presented, besides that of space, arose from the necessity of turning him around occasionally so the side away from the window would get some light. When an indoor avocado tree of this size is in one of its peak growing periods, the pot has to be turned a hundred and eighty degrees at least twice a week so the plant, in striving for light, doesn't become completely lopsided. Invariably, when turning Arthur's tub of dirt, I came close to getting a slipped disc.

This problem too was finally solved in the kitchen or, more accurately, in the dining room. One night when we had company, Susan served predinner canapés. Idly spinning the lazy Susan on which they reposed, and promising the next avocado tree to a guest, I had an idea. Later that evening, with the help of one of the dinner party and monumental effort we managed to slip the lazy Susan beneath Arthur's tub. The revolving tray broke beneath the strain. But later I located a suitably sturdy version, and it worked out very well.

On occasion I thought of motorizing the affair so the next plant that grew out of hand would turn quietly by itself at two rpw (revolutions per week). But even without a motor, a lazy Susan is a real back saver.

3

The Case of the Malingering Mango

The rescued mango pits mentioned in the Introduction brought down on my still budding horticultural career the greatest possible catastrophe—nothing happened. First thing in the morning for weeks on end I checked the soil in both pots carefully for signs of cracking or upheaval indicative of impending growth. But there was nary a sign of life. At last, in the second month, there did appear a small slender green shoot in the pot most exposed to sun—which wasn't very much, the window facing north. It was obviously a weed, at most grass or some other misrepresentative seed that had made its way into the mango pot. But I couldn't yank it out. After all . . .

This laissez-faire philosophy of plant growing, incidentally, early became a mainstay of my botanical endeavors, always producing interesting, if not necessarily enviable, results. As it turned out, it *was* some kind of grass that had sprouted. Two more months passed. I dug into the soil a bit to make sure the pits had not begun to rot. They were still there—big and firm, the beige flattish ovals somewhat resembling oversized dried lima beans, sitting stolidly on end in the soil, hard as nuts. One had been planted with the "eye"—indicating where the stem had held the fleshed fruit—down, the other with it up. I had a sneaking suspicion that was where the first growth would occur, but was not at all sure which way it should have pointed.

Three months passed, and I admit I was discouraged. Other things seemed to be sprouting or growing well by now. Lemon, orange, and grapefruit trees, two pineapples, and a pomegranate were rising lustily out of the earth. Arthur the avocado was getting almost out of hand. But still no mangoes.

The lack of response became even more frustrating when, driven at last to the library for research on dormant tendencies of this species, I discovered that the mango has been under successful cultivation for almost four thousand years in its native region of northeastern India, Burma, and Thailand. It seems the Mogul emperor Abkar, who reigned at Delhi in the late 1500s, was so taken with the mango's taste and fragrance that he had an orchard of over a hundred thousand trees laid out. This, spaced as mango trees properly are with thirty-five to forty feet between them, must have been quite a sight at a time when large fruit orchards were almost unheard of. Even today, I mused, it would be most impressive. We are used to the low spreading trees of temperate zone orchards, but the mango is a broad evergreen of deep dark shining foliage, reaching up as high as ninety feet. A whole plantation of this fruit—the apple of the tropics, as it is often called—would be something! However, all I wanted now was one sprout.

Wistfully reading on in search of clues, I found that the mango has a delightful family tree, including among its relatives pistachio and cashew nuts, as well as the Japanese lacquer. The black sheep of the family, poison ivy, might have worried me a little if anything had sprouted. But since there was still no sign of life, I discarded any possibility of the development of a throwback to this odious relative in my pot. It's well to note, however, that anyone sensitive to poison ivy should be on the lookout for reactions of a similar, but generally lesser, nature from handling or eating mangoes. The juice of the peel in particular can produce a rash; on the other hand, most people don't react to the juice of the pulp itself.

I did learn one reason I might be having such difficulty. The mango seed retains its viability for a relatively short time only. It seems that though for centuries the mango—with its strange, delicately flavored, brilliant orange fruit—was the delight of every Westerner who tasted it, the tree itself had not been grown outside its native region because the seeds would not remain fertile long enough to permit shipment elsewhere. The Western hemisphere, which had given the world so many fruits and vegetables, ranging from potatoes and corn to tomatoes and cocoa, didn't get the mango in return until the eighteenth century because the ships were too slow. Still, the time element shouldn't have affected my mangoes; they came by plane.

Impatient, but trying to use great care, I again scratched away some soil to check one of my pits—just as any experienced gardener would tell me not to do. A small crack seemed to be developing along that edge of the pit where the heaviest concentration of "hairs" or threads left from the fibrous fruit had been before. Was it just rotting? Or actively germinating?

Two weeks later I had my answer. A three-inch sprout, pale and skinny and bare, shooting up at the rate of almost half an inch a day. Of course it was the pit with the eye down, so the plant had had to grow in a complete "U" before surfacing, presumably taking twice as long as a pit planted eye up. Still, it had succeeded.

When the sprout was about four inches tall, the first tiny leaves, four of them all told, began to extend themselves in the form of a graceful crown at the apex. They were a surprising deep shiny crimson, delicate and drooping. As the leaves grew longer, these first ones to about three inches, they turned slowly and subtly dark green, at the same time hardening and losing their droop to arch out almost horizontally. With its long stem and crown of leaves, my mango in its early stage looked like a miniature palm.

A few mangoes later I came up with one that didn't look like a miniature palm, but a whole oasis of lopsided ones. I had four separate trunks coming out of one pit. I later found out that this type of "multiple mango" is not too infrequent. Although professionals recommend cutting back all but one of the shoots for maximum growth, leaving only one main trunk, I found that letting them develop their own split personalities added interest and variety.

The mango, I discovered quite by accident and much to my distress, is much more frost-sensitive than many other tropical or semitropical evergreens, such as citrus fruit. In the beginning, all my plants sat on the windowsill for maximum light, which even in wintertime seemed to do them no harm since the heat circulation throughout the apartment was quite thorough. Indeed, the warmth, according to Susan, was a real fringe benefit of my tropical gardening bug; before being bitten by it, I habitually slept with the windows open all winter. Still, even with the windows closed and carefully caulked against winter drafts, accidents will happen. One morning on my daily inspection I found all the leaves on the window side of the mango turning brown and shriveling up. I had been rotating the plant to coax it to grow straight—left to themselves on the sill, the plants all bend toward the light, threatening to become permanently deformed—and the leaves had come to rest on the cold glass and been frostbitten. I lost my first and favorite mango that way and had to start all over again.

Although my mango pits sometimes took four months to sprout, others began their growth in a matter of weeks. Even using the ripest fruit available, however, I was never able to get more than 75 percent of them to germinate.

The first thing to remember in cultivating mangoes is to remove the fruit from the pit as completely and carefully as possible, first scraping the pit with a knife and then using an old toothbrush and lukewarm water to scrub off what flesh re-

mains among the hairs. The hairs themselves will not come off and may be left for planting. If you're worried about a skin reaction, rubber gloves can be worn when cleaning the pits.

Once removed from the fruit, the pit should be left in a warmish spot to soak, fully covered with water, for about five days. Change the water every day, keeping it tepid, to avoid stagnation. After its baby bath, the pit is ready for planting, eye up, about half an inch below the surface of a very loose loamy soil. The seed should not be laid flat, but placed on end. If it lies flat, water tends to collect on top of it, sometimes inducing rotting instead of germination.

As with any seed, it's a must to water the mango very heavily on planting. The soil may in fact be allowed to turn almost to mud. After a few days, when the surface has begun to feel dry again, begin regular watering, using lukewarm water. Tepid water is almost always best; this is true not only for tropical plants, which are sensitive to cold, but, with rare exceptions, for potted plants in general.

In tropical countries plants may be showered every day during the rainy season. But nature supplies other conditions the great indoors does not. As a result, it's not the best idea to water plants or seeds every day, even if it seems more natural. One of the easiest absentminded habits the after-dinner gardener can slip into is overwatering. Usually twice a week is sufficient, except in a very dry apartment. I use an old teapot for watering. But, to avoid disturbing the soil and perhaps exposing roots close to the surface, I pour the water slowly around the edge of the pot. The soil should appear to readily absorb the moisture; under no circumstances should it become so wet that water is left standing on the surface. I supplement this regular procedure once every two weeks by watering from the bottom, pouring water into the drainage dish until it is no longer absorbed, then draining off the excess.

One of the few exceptions I ever made to this rule of thumb

in watering was the mango. A mango tree will not flower or fruit unless it goes through a "dry season" reminiscent of its native tropical environment, I learned. Although none of mine ever flowered—it takes about four years, and indoor mango plants probably never will—I took this bit of information to heart from the beginning, thinking the seasonal effect might also aid the mango's other stages of growth. I let the soil go dry for a week every month. Then I watered the plants quite heavily for the rest of the month. Which is not the way nature runs its wet and dry seasons, but my mangoes thrived on it.

Mangoes grow in spurts. After a dormant period of from four to six weeks, a new bunch of dark red leaves will suddenly crown a tree, hurriedly extend themselves to their proper slim length, which after the first year's growth of a plant is about eight inches, fading in the process to a pale rose-green, then gradually firming and darkening to blend in with the older leaves.

As for us, while we've found the mango one of the most attractive of indoor trees, due to a private impasse we've temporarily given up eating the fruit. Susan likes hers somewhat on the underripe side, whereas, since the seed is more apt to germinate when the fruit is completely ripened, I can't bear to waste pits by premature eating.

4

Pointers on Pineapples

The early mass distribution of the pineapple around the world can probably be attributed, in a very real sense, to numerous inadvertent after-dinner gardeners of a pioneer sort. On his second voyage in 1493, Columbus found the inhabitants of Guadeloupe eating what looked to him to be very curious fruits. At that time modern agriculture had not yet made a bigger and better pineapple than nature; the specimens Columbus saw reminded him of large pine cones. Hence the name, derived from the Spanish *piña*. Only fifty years later, Spanish and Portuguese sailing ships had carried pineapples all over the world, and they were under cultivation wherever the climate allowed—which, pineapples being not too particular, included lots of places. They took most enthusiastically to the Orient, or vice versa.

What permitted this unusually rapid spread of the pineapple—even by slow boat to China—was what also makes it an ideal after-dinner crop. For one thing, the vegetative parts of the plant are very resistant to drying out and wilting. They will withstand months of storage in a ship's hold or a supermarket's warehouse. Secondly, all it takes to start a pineapple plant is the crown, or top, of the fruit. Given a climate not actually hostile, pineapple plants sprouted wherever they were

eaten and their tops were relegated to the dump or, more likely, thrown heedlessly along the roadway or path after dinner.

Grown indoors, of course, the pineapple doesn't have the advantages of tropic skies. In the rarified stratosphere of an air-conditioned apartment, in fact, it might have a struggle against starvation if left untended. It likes atmosphere. But it's not so particular about its bed. It can have a fairly shallow pot; the roots of the pineapple do not grow deep. The soil to plant it in is no problem, either.

The mixture for a pineapple is straight from the kitchen. At least in part. Ever since the budget stopped calling for using the coffee grounds twice, I've wondered if there weren't some use to which they could be put. We drink an awful lot of coffee, despite resolutions to cut down our caffeine intake. And the plumber long ago disposed of one of Susan's most stubbornly cherished old household remedies, namely pouring grounds down the sink drain to prevent its clogging. It was on that same visit that he also gave me a lecture on roots, pebbles, and other vagrants from the garden in the kitchen sink trap.

Coffee grounds are high in acid. If there's one thing pine-apples love, it's rich organic acidic soil. Putting two and two together, I decided on a soil mixture of half potting soil, a quarter humus, and a quarter coffee grounds. Before they are used as a planting medium, the coffee grounds should be rinsed until the water running through them comes out fairly clear. Then they should be thoroughly dried. Baking them on a cookie tin until well done is much preferable to spreading them out on a newspaper to dry. Or so I've been told by Susan, who feels we already have enough things drying on assorted spread-out newspapers all over the place. Besides which, drying them in the oven, while it doesn't give the effect roasting original beans does, still adds a cosy aroma to the kitchen.

The green top of the pineapple is what you lob off for plant-ing, taking about an inch of the fruit with it. Let it rest a day or two before planting, then bury the fruit slice so the soil comes right up to the bottom of the crown. To set a cutting properly, I give it a good heavy watering. Also, since discovering liquid fertilizer, I spray a weak dilution of it on the crown the first day of planting, to help speed up initial growth.

This somewhat strange application of fertilizer is very important to the pineapple because of its esoteric family tree. Originating in the Matto Grosso region of Brazil and Paraguay, the pineapple belongs to the family of Bromeliaceae, all of whose members are native to Latin America except Spanish moss, which, perversely, is native to the west coast of Africa. Most of the Bromeliaceae are epiphytic plants—sometimes known as "air plants" because they take their nourishment not from the soil but from substances dissolved in the rain or dew. Epiphytic plants like orchids and mosses quite often cling to the bark of living trees high up from the jungle floor, without feasting on their host the way a parasite would. Others, including some lichens, grow on the ground, but again do not take their sustenance from it.

The pineapple does grow roots, properly delving down into the soil. But they are shallow, and not as effective as the leaves in gathering nutriments. Although not a true epiphytic plant anymore, the pineapple still absorbs dissolved material in dew, rain, or home-bottled spray falling on its leaves more readily than anything spoon-fed to its roots.

While we had no air-conditioning to deprive our pineapples of access to normal air, and city water has goodness knows what in it anymore, I still worried about undernourishment. Commercial growers dose their pineapple plants with enough fertilizer to remain in the crown for some time, and I decided to do the same. That's how I mutilated my first two pineapple plants. Although it's an excellent, almost essential, way to foster their growth, in my enthusiasm I neglected the old saw about too much of a good thing. The fertilizer, about a thimbleful, was too strong for the tender crown, and proceeded to burn all the tiny new leaves. They came up brown and wilted at their points, though they were extraordinarily healthy the rest of the way down. The mature leaves that made up the crown had holes burned right through them.

One of the plants stopped growing altogether. A month later I stopped beside it on my jungle rounds, idly wondering what first aid I could possibly give it, and suddenly noticed a bright green nob, looking for all the world like a dunce's cap, poking out from under a bushy brim of leaves. The plant had decided to give up on the crown and sent out a new shoot, which thrived.

This procedure is quite a normal one for pineapple plants even when they haven't been overdosed with fertilizer. Such shoots are of two main types: the ratoon, which comes out beneath the soil and develops its own root system; and the aerial sucker, which even by W. C. Fields's standards doesn't get an even break, having no roots at all. Both the ratoon and the aerial sucker can be separated from the parent pineapple once they have developed half a dozen healthy leaves. The ratoon, needless to say, will have a head start on planting.

My experience with liquid fertilizer needn't deter you from spraying your pineapples. Just be sure you keep the solution you use to a fourth or less the recommended strength. For instance, if the instructions are to add two spoonfuls of fertilizer to a given amount of water, add only half a spoonful. But water each pineapple well and make sure the crown gets a thorough dousing. Try to avoid a fertilizer high in phosphates; the pineapple doesn't take well to them. And if you want to feel like a real pro, read the ingredients given for available fertilizers and select one that relies on an ammonium compound, rather than a sodium one, for nitrogen.

Many of our friends, trying to start a pineapple top at home, complain that it just sits there, green as ever but not growing

anywhere. Usually the problem is that the pineapple is suffering, as it does readily, from iron deficiency anemia, otherwise known as "tired sap." A little extra iron makes a noticeable difference. I used to put old staples and broken tacks in the soil, thinking they would rust in no time and supply all the iron the plant could want. Not so. Although rusting tacks and staples can eventually make available the kind of iron pineapple roots can swallow, the complex chemical process involved takes a long time and can't always be counted on to occur when you want it to. My pineapples sat on their bed of nails, not rising an inch.

Then one day at the local florist's I discovered and immediately pounced upon a packet of plant food containing "instant" available iron. It really did the trick. I took to using it generously and fairly frequently (about once a month) on my pineapples and, for that matter, every once in a while on all the other plants, to supplement regular fertilization. For best results with pineapples—as witness my enthusiastic blunder—dilute it to about a fourth the recommended strength and apply it with a spray bottle to the leaves and particularly the crown. Watch closely for browning and other signs of fertilizer burn. Burning a leaf, or even the crown itself, will rarely kill the plant, but it does make it less attractive.

Under outdoor cultivation, a crown cutting is supposed to mature and bear in twenty-four to thirty months. Apartment-bound pineapple plants tend to take longer, if they bear at all. But I have seen pineapples, if diminutive ones, grown indoors. The pineapple, incidentally, is a multiple fruit. The flowers, a hundred or more, grow clustered on a spike rising from the crown. When they are fertilized, they fuse together to form what we know as the pineapple itself.

Even without its fruit, the pineapple is an interesting and decorative plant. The variety sold in supermarkets is the "Smooth Cayenne," which luckily, as the name implies, doesn't have the sharp sawtooth edges of the wilder species. It is adaptable to varying conditions. Although these pineapples like lots of sunshine once they have rooted, I've grown them successfully with no direct sunlight at all. But should you have hopes for their fruiting, they will need many hours of sunlight a day and a constant temperature between seventy-five and eighty-five degrees Fahrenheit. Below sixty-five degrees the plant, thinking it's in cold storage, will become dormant, ceasing to grow. Much above ninety degrees it suffers from a case of excessive transpiration and respiration; that is to say, it sweats profusely and feels it's just too hot to do anything.

Actually you might be better off if your pineapple doesn't fruit. You won't be so tempted to lob off the top of your very own homegrown pineapple—and the next, and the next—to keep the home chain growing. It's easier somehow to force yourself to throw out the tops of supermarket Smooth Cayennes. And things *can* get out of hand. One may keep eating pineapples indefinitely, if one likes them—but all those sproutable spiny tops! In the Philippines they've been making a fine *piña* cloth from the fiber of the leaves since the 1600s. I don't know how they do it, but someday I intend to go and find out. One can accumulate too many pineapple plants scrambling over one's window ledge.

5

The Chinese Gooseberry

I've been a gooseberry gourmet since childhood, when I spent many a summer afternoon popping them between my teeth so the sun-warmed, sour insides squirted out. You seldom see them in the city. Even when you do find them, they're not up to snuff. Thus when I peered into a new crate at the local fruit stand, labeled CHINESE GOOSEBERRIES, and saw gooseberries the size of extra-large jumbo eggs, I was overwhelmed.

Of course they didn't look quite right. Apart from their incredible size, these were olive-gray, not light translucent green; their skin was leathery instead of crisp; and the brown tuft at the end was far too small. Besides, who ever heard of paying forty-nine cents for *two* gooseberries. Still, inevitably, two accompanied me home.

Cutting one in half, I decided it looked like a miniature but bright chartreuse watermelon, with dark brown seeds the size of pinheads running in ribs along its center. The taste, however, is a delight which can be conjured up only by eating another one.

As was so often to happen, I had on my hands the problem of trying to find out what we'd eaten and why it was called what it was. There is a tree in the East Indies, the Carambola, which, according to *A Dictionary of Trees*, is supposedly called the Chinese gooseberry tree. It grows to a height of twenty-

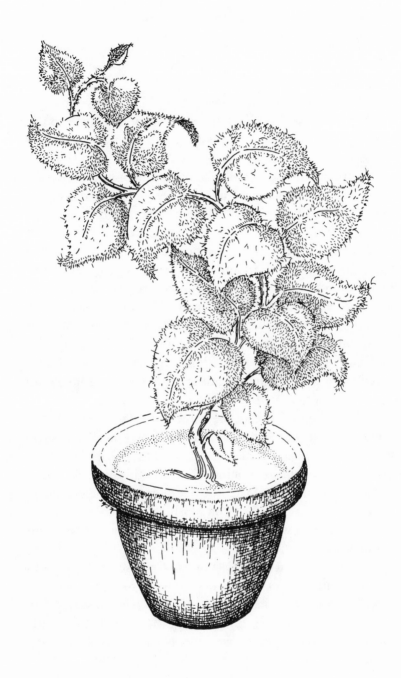

five feet and bears an oval fruit three to four inches long, usually with five longitudinal ribs forming star-shaped sections when the fruit is sliced crosswise. The fruit was described as bright yellow instead of bright green. A dubious relative.

Nevertheless, I couldn't find any description closer to what we'd eaten, and it was the only reference at all to "Chinese gooseberry." Of course it didn't explain where either the "gooseberry" or the "Chinese" came from, or how they got together, and I must admit I was thoroughly confused geographically, since I had noticed the crate I got ours from had come from New Zealand.

My only hope was that maybe if I grew the plant it would give me some clue. Carefully picking out the tiny seeds with a knife point, I spread them on a blotter to dry for a couple of days. Since the seeds were so incredibly small, it seemed logical the roots would be, too. I decided on a very loose mixture, two-thirds humus and one-third soil, with a handful of vermiculite. Laying the dried seeds gently on top of the soil, I covered them with another eighth of an inch or so of humus and gave them a thorough watering to settle them in.

The "Chinese" half of the name must have got there for a reason, I argued; accordingly, having always pictured China as a country of plentiful sunshine, I stuck the pot in the sunniest corner. My absurd reasoning worked in this case. Sometimes I haven't been so fortunate . . . but more of that later. Chinese gooseberry plants do thrive on sunshine, although you can also grow them in a window with as little as an hour of direct sunlight a day.

The description of the East Indian Chinese gooseberry I had found indicated not only that it grew up to be a proper tree, but that it adorned itself in compound leaves consisting of up to eleven small smooth leaflets along the main stem. I waited. My seeds germinated in eight weeks, and proceeded to grow ever larger and larger heart-shaped leaves, coated with a delicate silver fur. As they continued to climb, they wandered up into vines. Definitely not trees. Obviously I wasn't the only confused one around. My plants had no idea what they were supposed to look like, either.

I was momentarily at a loss. Then one day I spotted another crate of Chinese gooseberries, this one downtown. The only difference was the label—KIWI FRUIT. The crate, consistently enough, came from New Zealand.

Rummaging around with New Zealand in mind, I finally found the answer, in a bulletin from their Department of Agriculture, to the riddle of the Chinese gooseberry. To begin with, it originated in the mild-wintered Yangtze Valley of China. There it grows as a wild semitropical vine, often reaching a height of thirty feet or more in the forest. Under cultivation, it is grown in arbors, much as grapevines are. The fruit hangs down ready for picking, just like grapes except it grows singly rather than in bunches.

Although the fruit—and because of their size I still can't think of them as berries—we had eaten came from New Zealand, their origin explained at least the first half of their name. Where the "gooseberry" part came from I never did find out.

Gooseberries, smooshberries, the thing is they make very good eating, and lovely plants as well. Easy to grow, their one weakness as seedlings—in common with other "watery-stemmed" plants, as opposed to woody trees—is a proneness to "damping off." This fungus disease kills the tissue cells at a point where the stem of a plant enters the earth. The stem becomes brown and shriveled at soil level. Then the plant just tips over and dies. All young plants are susceptible to damping off, in varying degrees; the Chinese gooseberry is particularly sensitive. Once it has struck there isn't much you can do. By being certain the soil you use in the first place is sterilized, you can minimize the chance of its occurrence. But should it strike in one pot, it will spread, so either dispose of the soil or re-sterilize it.

My second batch of Chinese gooseberry seeds didn't seem to be interested in sprouting. I discovered that this could be due to their having missed their winter vacation. In a magazine *not* lying on the table in my dentist's waiting room, I found an article entitled "The Effects of Stratification and Alternating Temperatures on Seed Germination of *Actinidia chinensis.*" The gist of it was that the Chinese gooseberry had a better chance of germinating if it went through a period of "after-ripening." In its natural environment, a certain type of seed goes through a period between the time it falls to the ground in autumn and its germination the following spring when it is covered by de-caying fruit, leaves, snow, etc. When both moisture and a cool temperature are necessary for this after-ripening, the process is called "stratification."

With this in mind, I stuck the next pot of incipient Chinese gooseberries, well watered beneath their blanket of humus, on the bottom shelf of our refrigerator. As I went back to my newspaper, Susan commented from the kitchen.

"You know, of course, the light goes off when we shut the door. "

"What light?"

She slammed the refrigerator door.

"That one."

"So?" I answered.

"So how's it going to grow without any light?"

"How's what going to grow without any light?"

"The icicle," she giggled.

Rattling my paper firmly, I replied:

"I'm *not* growing icicles."

"Well, what's that pot doing in the icebox, then?"

"Stratifying," I said simply.

The process of stratification takes four to six weeks, during which the temperature should not fall below about forty degrees Fahrenheit. No change will be observable. However, inside the seed changes are taking place that will break its dormancy. A month had passed when Susan suggested that winter might be over; she needed the refrigerator shelf. I put the pot in the window, and in two weeks about half the seeds had sprouted, a considerable improvement over the last batch.

By nature the Chinese gooseberry is a deciduous plant, shedding its leaves in the fall to sprout new ones the next spring. Indoors, though, mine stayed green all year round, the old leaves waiting till the new ones unfolded before dropping to the ground, keeping the window they framed always adorned.

You may be the first in your neighborhood to have Chinese gooseberry vines covering up a window with big, soft, fuzzy leaves, but the fruit itself is probably appearing in one form or another on tables up and down the block, as it has gained in popularity since its reconsideration as kiwi fruit. It's a very healthy fruit, containing in its small self as much vitamin C as an equivalent-sized orange. And although I suspect there would be some consumer resistance to drinking green juice for breakfast, its other uses are many: jellies, jams, pies, a touch of color in nouvelle cuisine, and of course East Indian Chinese Gooseberry Chutney.

6

How Sweet It Is . . .

A nice blend of vines and trees was developing in my jungle. But I began to feel a definite need for something grassy or reedy to lend a little space and lightness to what could turn into a rather dense undergrowth. I'd been dreaming fruitlessly about a bamboo grove for some time; the canned shoots sold in our neighborhood, their name notwithstanding, couldn't be expected to sprout.

Then, foraging around in a Spanish greengrocer's one day, I almost passed up a tall stack of green-topped red canes. Odd-looking bamboo, I thought to myself as I headed for the banana bunches, intent on finding some wild ones with potential seeds. On the way back I stopped for a closer look at the poles. It dawned on me—sugarcane. Of course!

Now what I didn't know about sugarcane could fill several volumes. Obviously one couldn't just stick it into a pot and have it grow. Still, never having had real sugarcane, I couldn't resist buying a few stalks.

I took it home—all eight feet of it—on the subway and gave it a real scrutiny. It was divided into segments, just like bamboo, if less pronounced. But what riveted my attention was a small shield-shaped scale on one side of each joint. Hmm, vaguely possible that a bud lurked beneath that. Just below the scale the joint, or node, was circled by a double row of pin-sized dots on a small light-colored band.

"Now," I asked aloud, "if I were a piece of sugarcane, and I had a bud, what would those dots be?" And with a smile I answered myself, "Incipient roots, of course."

Meanwhile Susan had discovered my find and was happily occupied peeling back cane and chewing one chunk after another. She was halfway through the second eight-foot cane when I rescued it from her clutches.

"Oh no, I'm going to plant this one."

She eyed our ceiling with an obvious air of doubt, sucking absently on a long-since dry hunk of cane.

"Mmm?" was all she said aloud.

I cut off a complete section, or internode, of the cane, leaving it enclosed by a joint at each end. Then I stuck it in a pot filled with one-third humus and two-thirds potting soil. I sank it so the lower node, or joint, was just below the surface. If those pinpoints were indeed where the roots would emerge, they would emerge into nice homey soil. Any young roots are sensitive. If they came out above ground level, chances were they would dry out and die.

I did scratch back the surface soil right around the shield— just so I could see if anything was happening. Then I had another thought. Since the cane was a sliced-off section, it might become dehydrated. Borrowing a candle from the dining room table, I dripped wax onto the top until it was sealed off.

At morning inspection the next day, the shield seemed to be distinctly bigger. I called Susan over. She looked at it dutifully, shook her head, and went back to the kitchen. Next to my breakfast coffee was a large bowl of sugar cubes, labeled JUST IN CASE.

"Some people have no faith," I grumbled, putting four lumps into my coffee by mistake. I drank it anyhow.

41

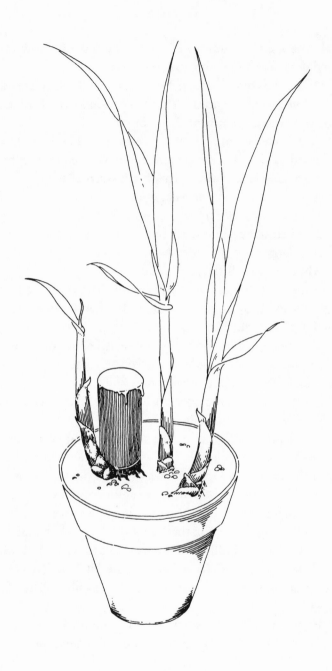

Next day the shield was definitely larger. There was no denying it, but I refrained from comment. A week later the shield parted from the stalk, and the bud itself poked its head out from under it. I had sugarcane growing in my window.

The ancients must have had a pretty sweet life, even without saccharin. Or perhaps I should say *with* it. Sugar cane belongs to the genus *Saccharum* and has been under cultivation in India since as early as 400 B.C. Even in those days it was milled and made into sugar by a simple process of heating and drying that is still in use in lesser developed areas today. From India sugarcane was carried to China, Arabia, and Southern Europe and the Mediterranean. In the early 1400s it was introduced into the Azores and Madeira, where it did so well as a cash crop—that is, one sold for profit rather than being consumed by the grower—that it entirely eliminated the Mediteranean industry.

Here Columbus enters the horticultural picture once more; he took some with him on his second voyage to Hispaniola. From there it spread rapidly to Cuba and Puerto Rico, then to Mexico and on down to Peru and Brazil. The sugarcane that made its way throughout South America, however, was rather thin and anemic compared with today's variety.

Modern sugarcane originally came from the South Seas, most probably New Guinea. Captain Bligh sailed with a cargo of *Saccharum officinarum,* the official sugarcane of today's industry, from Tahiti on his 1791 voyage. Apparently even the cargo hold of sugarcane didn't sweeten him enough for the crew, since they told him to go row his own boat. But that was after he had delivered the cane to Jamaica. Its superior quality was undeniably evidenced by the fact that it was much thicker, containing more raw sugar. It soon replaced all other varieties.

The fact that he had taken aboard whole cane intrigued me. Why not just seeds? The reason, I discovered, was that Captain Bligh was one up on me. True sugarcane seeds are never used for planting. For one thing, they grow very slowly. For another, the seeds are heterogeneous: that is, they do not breed true to their parents, producing instead countless spurious varieties. Thirdly, some varieties don't even bother to flower, and thus have no seeds.

Just to be contrary, the standard planting material of the sugarcane *is* called a "seed." But this seed is actually a stem cutting like the one I used. The planting method of commercial growers is different in that they don't cover a whole field with little cuttings sticking halfway up out of the ground like mine. They make long furrows and bury them. This can be done by the after-dinner gardener, too, by laying the cutting in a pot, the bud on one side, and covering it with about an inch of soil. The bud sprouts more quickly this way, and the young plant is more firmly anchored, an advantage because of its eventual tall skinniness.

Since I felt the old sugarcane stalk from which the shoot would arise added something to the overall picture, I continued to stick some of mine halfway into the pot and wax over the exposed cut ends. Once a new shoot reached a height of four or five inches, I added another inch or so of loose soil, a precaution against its getting top-heavy and tipping over.

The fresher a cane, the more likely it is to sprout. Also, cuttings halfway up the cane seem to be the best for after-dinner planting, probably because the middle has not yet been affected by the drying out that starts in on the cut ends. If you ever have difficulty coaxing a sugarcane to sprout, take a new cutting and let it sit under cold running water, or in frequently changed cold water, for about twenty-four hours. This will break the dormancy of the buds and not only induce some to sprout that wouldn't otherwise, but also make all of them sprout more quickly.

A cane cutting won't stop at a single stalk. It will produce several, sometimes up to five or six. They will stand high in their pot looking very much like a clump of reddish bamboo with slightly too many of the wrong kind of green leaves.

Well, until I managed to get some bamboo shoots capable of sprouting, my clump of canes would have to do. Meanwhile, Susan came up with an intriguing way of using sugarcane. She started serving individual sticks made from center sections of the cane with coffee. You just stir until the brew is sweetened to taste.

7

Please Lower the Floor,
and Other Problems with Avocados

Arthur, my first avocado tree, shot up, straight up—a broom-
stick with leaves. When he was four feet tall there was but a
single trunk, leaves along its entire length. For a tree, the avocado is a fairly fast-growing specimen, but by the time Arthur
reached the stage of needing a lazy Susan to turn him around
on, so heavy was his tub becoming, I began to wonder how
long this was going to go on.

Finally, when he was six feet tall, branches shot out about a
foot below the crown. Barely in time. We had nine-foot ceilings, and I was figuring the odds on which would give first—
floor, ceiling, or Arthur.

The branches grew, but they drooped, ducking the top of
the window, I thought, to get enough light. Arthur acquired a
sad, baggy, stoop-shouldered appearance. It was not until my
next avocado spread out its first branches in the same sagging
fashion that I learned it's the natural posture of an unpruned
avocado tree.

Susan's folks had previously expressed an interest in the avocado. Their house sat on a sunny knoll. It also had higher ceilings than ours; Arthur would no doubt feel less cramped living
with them. Regretfully we decided to relocate him.

As they lived in Pennsylvania, this presented certain new
problems, not the least of which was that we didn't keep a tall

car in the city. A train, we decided, had the highest ceiling on wheels.

Balancing Arthur on a skateboard, we rolled him down to the street corner and hailed a taxi. I opened the door and began to coax him in. The driver turned quickly with a mumbled "Sorry, I didn't realize the tree was with you," and drove off.

Several cabs later we managed to get a ride to Penn Station. I left Susan parked with the tree on the boarding platform while I went to get the tickets, just to make sure the ticket agent didn't try to sell me a third one. The ride down was uneventful, except that the conductor looked somewhat askance at me as I stood beneath the shade of our tree in the passageway, observing the passing avocadoless landscape.

Arthur moved out to the patio that summer. There he thrived. So much so, in fact, he couldn't be gotten back into the house. With fall and chilly evenings approaching, there seemed to be no solution to his housing problem except to send him off to school. He moved to the local junior high to become a permanent member of the biology class.

Avocados came in with the jet set. Although long a favorite staple in much of Central and South America, they did not gain popular recognition in the temperate and northern zones until modern transportation gave them wings. They were too perishable. But once they got air cargo space, they took over. They flocked from Mexico, the West Indies, Guatemala, and then, inevitably, from California and Florida.

The "alligator pear," as the avocado used to be known before it was decided that such a nomenclature was not conducive to mass promotion, is one of the most prized of tropical fruits. Discounting for the moment the now ubiquitous citrus fruits, the avocado is usually ranked just below the banana, pineapple, and mango as a tropical fruit crop.

I never expected my pits to yield a real crop, but I did toy with the idea of at least supplying the family larder eventually.

After all, for the after-dinner plantation, avocados are a natural. For the most part the avocado pit or seed germinates readily. The plant itself is not too choosy about sun and soil, and produces a luxuriant bush or tree. When I first started growing avocados—that was before Arthur hit the ceiling—I thought my biggest problem was going to be simply deciding which variety I wanted most.

There are two main species of avocado from which most cultivated varieties derive. *Persea americana*, which originated in Guatemala and the West Indies, has a thick leathery skin and can be easily distinguished from its thin-skinned Mexican relative, *Persea drymifolia*. The leaves of the latter give off an odor of anise when crushed; the former are odorless. But then there are the hybrids, the Fuerte, for instance, apparently a cross between the Mexican and the Guatemalan. There are spring varieties, like Spinks, Blakeman, and Lyon; summer varieties, like Dickinson and Taft; fall and winter varieties; and so on.

The further I delved into the subject of avocados, looking for a propagation-minded variety, the more confused I became. The nice, simple two-system classification with which everyone started out had somehow gotten lost in a hopeless mass of hybrids and variants. Popenoe's *Manual of Tropical and Subtropical Fruits: Excluding the Banana, Coconut, Pineapple, Citrus Fruits, Olive, and Fig*, an early classic in the field published in 1920, mentioned more than a hundred and fifty varieties in the United States alone—and that was before the avocado was popularized. With American agriculturists constantly striving for bigger and more beautiful fruit, who knows how many varieties there are now?

Basically all the after-dinner gardener needs to know, I decided finally, is that the avocado picked out of the grocer's basket is most probably from either Florida or California, and that it makes a difference. Florida avocados are usually larger, their skin rougher and darker than the California ones. Their flesh

is softer, containing more oil than those from California, and the pit is proportionately smaller. Aside from these characteristics, the two can usually be differentiated simply by their shape. The Florida variety must have been the origin of the name "alligator pear." Not only does its rough skin imitate that of the alligator, if you squint at it very hard, but it is truly pear-shaped. The California avocado, on the other hand, is much rounder, almost oval in appearance. Without wanting to get caught in the middle of the perennial chamber of commerce combat between Florida and California, in all honesty I have to note from my experience that the Florida variety germinates much more readily, grows more quickly, and is usually much tastier besides.

I had heard that in Guatemala, from which the best wild avocados come, four or five tortillas served with avocado are considered by many an unexcelled meal. So Susan went out for corn meal and mixed up a tortilla batter while I dug out the pits. She really wanted to serve soup Guatemalan-style. There one is served a big bowl of soup with an avocado next to it. One cuts open the avocado at the table and scoops it out into the hot soup. But I had visions of somebody's pit dropping into the soup—they're very slippery—and being scalded beyond all hope of sprouting. I vetoed the soup idea. Later we took to eating our avocados simply as guacamole, served in salads, or stuffed with shrimp or Mandarin orange slices.

We always pick our avocados from the fruit stand as ripe as we can find, ideally, slightly soft to the touch. The pit of a very ripe avocado is sometimes so eager to sprout that it's already begun by the time the fruit is opened. Halve an avocado gently, by the way, working in from the outside in a circle to avoid slicing through the pit. Where a pit has already sprouted prior to eviction, it should be rinsed off in tepid water and planted immediately.

Where, as is more often the case, the pit is a tight brown-skinned nut, showing no pale shoot between its halves, rinse it off in tepid water, pat it dry with a soft towel, and let it sit in a warm dry spot for a day, or overnight. I reserved a comfortable kitchen corner, the one formerly saved for rising bread, as a matter of fact, for my avocado pits. After the pit has dried off for a day, the parchmentlike skin surrounding it can be easily peeled away. If, as occasionally happens, this coat is shed as you remove the pit from the fruit, you can skip the drying period and plant it right away.

Some home avocado growers advocate sticking toothpicks into the pit and balancing it precariously, partially submerged, across a glass of water. For a first avocado, this is more interesting in that you can watch the roots develop. But if the object is results, the toothpick procedure is more trouble than it's worth. Sometimes the water goes sour, which means not only throwing the pit away, but having a miniature swamp on your hands. Another worry is possible injury to the roots in transferring the plant from glass to pot.

The simplest method is to plant the pit directly in the pot in which it is to grow. One with a diameter of seven inches or so is ideal for the first year's growth. Layer the bottom of the pot as with your other plants, then fill it with a mixture of two-thirds potting soil and one-third humus, adding a handful of vermiculite. Avocados will grow in almost any soil, but do best in heavy, moist loam.

Once I got over my initial fear of injuring young pits, I adopted the practice, recommended by the California Experiment Station, of cutting a thin sliver off both tip and base of the seed, using a single-edged razor blade. The slivers should be no more than an eighth of an inch thick. This surgery isn't essential, but I found it helps speed germination.

An avocado pit is planted base (the larger, flatter end, usually slightly indented) down, buried about two-thirds into the soil so that the tip is still well exposed. Part of the pit must have access to light; otherwise it will not germinate. According to investigations conducted by scientists at the U.S. Department of Agriculture in Beltsville, Maryland, this light requirement is probably due to action on a pigment, called *phytochrome*, in the seed. However, most of their research in the field was done on Grand Rapids lettuce seeds. The workings of the light-sensitive mechanism are so esoteric, and the research so inconclusive, that—aside from unearthing the mistletoe's need to germinate in the dark, obvious even to amateurs—I've not been able to come up with anything more definite than that some seeds need light to germinate and others don't. Avocados do.

As soon as it's nestled in, the pit should be doused with tepid water. If the air in your apartment is very dry, invert a clear plastic cup or glass over the pit to help keep moisture in the soil around it. Then sit back and wait about a month for the seed to split, the first sign of germination. Few of my avocado pits have failed to germinate at all, but some have taken as long as three months to sprout, so be patient. While it sits there looking innocent, the pit is most likely building a good subterranean root system before it makes any growing noises aboveground.

Once the first sprout of avocado does emerge from the splitting seed and reaches a height of four inches or so, add another layer of humus, between half an inch and an inch, to cover the pit. The avocado has roots that come close to the surface for nourishment, and they are easily injured by dry soil or sun. The extra layer of humus will ensure sufficient moisture for best growth.

Every time one of my avocados reached a height of six inches or so, I began having troubled dreams about Arthur again. To prune or not to prune? That is the question. In nature, of course, a young tree is rarely pruned, and then only by accident, when a passing animal tramples the plant or decides to lunch on the tender young leaves. People, however, are incurable improvers upon nature even if their "improvements" sometimes turn out to be duds. Avocado trees in commercial groves are carefully grafted, as well as pruned, to produce the biggest, most disease-resistant, easiest-to-pick avocados. As fruits of "better and better" design are developed, I strongly suspect them of having less and less taste. Another reason for growing my own, I reminded myself. Still, the fact remains that a pruned tree tends to be stronger and better shaped.

The avocados I pruned remained more sensible than Arthur in their proportions. In fact they were "shaped" to fit specific nooks of the room. Tall and slender for floor models. Short and bushy for those on bookshelves or tables.

An avocado is often first cut back when the shoot is about six inches tall. Trim two inches off the top, making a clean diagonal sweep of it. The plant will then look rather barren and hopeless, but in a short while, usually a week or two, a new shoot will develop lower along the stem. New branches will lengthen more slowly than the original sprout, but they should be sturdier and grow more leaves.

Later, when the plant has grown to two or three feet in height, the new top can be pruned again. As smaller branches develop, they may be pruned to "force" out more branches. In general, the more you prune, the thicker and bushier your plant will grow. It's almost as if, being frustrated in one direction, the avocado fights back with all it's got on other fronts, more determined than ever.

A branch may be pruned off entirely if it gets too long or scraggly. The main trunk, however, should not normally be cut back more than a third of its height, although this process may be repeated over and over again.

Since it is one of the faster-growing tropical trees, as opposed, for instance, to the mango, the avocado will need a larger pot with seasonal regularity. Don't transplant it too often, but the plant's height should not exceed the diameter of its pot by more than six times—unless you're purposely trying to stunt the plant, to keep it within manageable limits. In that case, continue to cut it back and give it plenty of fertilizer, in lieu of the new and improved acreage it's missing out on.

Even if you do want to stunt a plant by keeping it in a small pot, it's a good practice to replant it every two years or so. Remove it from its quarters, delicately work out as much old soil from between the roots as you can with a dull pencil, or a sharp chopstick, and then repot it in a same-sized pot, using a fresh soil mixture.

For large pots I've found the large five-gallon plastic shortening buckets from restaurants quite handy. There are also a number of attractive commercial "tubs" made from redwood. Whatever you choose, remember that the avocado prefers a rich, loamy soil.

Since potting soil can be expensive in quantities large enough to fill a shortening bucket, I took to using regular soil from a country cousin's garden, supplementing it with fertilizer. However, I soon discovered that regular garden soil tends to pack when confined to large pots. So we started eating peanuts, bought in the shell, a few weeks before transplanting time came due. After a good case of indigestion, I'd usually accumulated enough peanut shells to mix in liberally with the soil. They make a good mulch, and as time goes on their decay leaves the soil loamy so the avocado roots have romping room.

As for coaxing fruit from even a large indoor avocado tree, however, I gave up on that idea quite early in the game. Even Arthur, a veteran of summer camp, never bore fruit, I've been told. Realistically speaking, I've learned since my early plantation dreams, it is highly improbable that a housebound avocado will. The indoor gardener just can't supply the conditions a tree needs to flower and bear. Friends farther south have set trees out for the summer, sometimes getting them to bloom and even produce some stunted fruit.

Myself, I came to the conclusion it would probably always be easier to buy avocados than wait for my Arthurs to oblige by one-upping my friends' trees. Besides, with the head start avocados had on the more esoteric or difficult tropical fruits converging on the country, there is enough of them to go around and then some. Which is perhaps why new guises for avocados are cropping up all over. South American Indians are reputed to rub avocado pulp into their scalps to prevent baldness, and cosmetic manufacturers in the United States are making extensive use of the avocado. Not as a talisman against baldness—at least not yet—but in a variety of more subtle, but equally effective, beauty aids calling for an oil base. Avocado oil is one of the finest and most delicate of the natural vegetable oils. Manufacturers in other fields are experimenting with its use, and one can occupy oneself quite a while guessing what they'll come up with.

Meanwhile, back in the culinary field—where I really feel the luscious pear belongs—I've been noticing lately a veritable outbreak of avocado recipes. So don't be surprised if one of these days that nice pistachio-colored ice cream you bring home turns out to be a popular Brazilian import and not among Baskin-Robbins's flavors—namely, avocado ice cream.

8

Lots of Yams, Please, I'm Not on a Diet

Early in the game, waiting restlessly for my jungle to overgrow the window, I reactivated one of my childhood rainy-day standbys, sprouting sweet potato vines. In the process I discovered modern science had struck again since I was a boy. More and more sweet potatoes and yams are now sprayed with a growth inhibitor to prevent unseemly sprigs from making their appearance on crops left unpicked along the grocer's shelves. Needless to say, this treatment also discourages them from growing in the garden when wanted.

Like many of us in North America, Susan is a sometime dieter. So when I went out and bought several pounds each of yams and sweet potatoes, she retreated behind her calorie counter, emitting ominous rumbles, which I think did not originate in an empty stomach. Of course since a whole yam or potato is used for the garden, one doesn't have to eat it at all. But one can't plant a whole peck of potatoes in one window.

Throwing in the towel, Susan served candied yams for a week running. That, she maintained, ought to take care of my sweet tooth for the next year. By the end of the week and the third bag of potatoes, I was fully satisfied that at least one of the lot was free of growth inhibitors. I had an uneasy sensation that I might sprout little candied yam sprigs if I ate any more.

Not only are many potatoes sprayed with growth inhibitors,

they are dyed as well. This I discovered when I went to wash those saved for planting. I found myself deluged in orange-red dye. Susan assured me they were not synthetic yams. I wasn't completely convinced, though I had to admit such a radical "improvement" as a plastic potato did seem a bit premature even for the most progressive American consumer specialists.

I sank my yam and my sweet potato, sans dye, in wide-mouthed applesauce jars partly filled with water—not without misgivings about the appropriateness of fruit jars for root crops. They worked fine. A week after the partial immersion, small green shoots began to appear. They were a big encouragement during the long wait for some of the slower jungle seeds to germinate; for instance, my date pits had been molding for nigh on six months . . . but later for that.

Once the main shoots were about eight inches high, I transplanted the potatoes to pots. I learned the hard way to bury them completely in soil, even if some of the vines sprouting every which way out of the tubers had to be covered with loose soil. Leaving a tuber exposed will produce an excellent serial documentary on rotting potato. Not to mention the hordes of small invaders likely to drop by.

Actually the tubers can be buried before they sprout at all. It will merely take longer to see results—which, when you're not sure whether or not you have an inhibited yam, could pose a problem.

There is a school of thought that "contrary thinking" is generally the most productive. In the case of the after-dinner garden this proves true quite frequently. Probably the best example of all is the sweet potato or the yam. In their natural habitat, their preference is for light, loose soil, in the line of a sandy loam that isn't too rich. Under this sort of roof the tubers produced will be golden, delicious, and many. On the other hand, if the soil is heavier and, relatively speaking, overly rich, the yam and sweet potato will produce a poor underground crop, concentrating more on putting out a lush green growth. With a going price of twenty-nine cents a pound for yams in our neighborhood, I was much more interested in growing the vines than harvesting the crop. So I used a rich potting mixture, half humus, half potting soil, with just a couple of small handfuls of sand for good measure.

The pots for yam or sweet potato vines should be deep, at least 50 percent deeper than the length of the tubers themselves. Like all quick-growing plants, they favor a liberal amount of water—I let mine lap up a drink three times a week or more—and, if they are kept in a sunny spot, overwatering shouldn't be much of a problem. While happiest with a sunny ledge to bake on, the plants will grow well enough on an hour or so of sunshine a day.

Given fairly sunny conditions, the vines on reaching maturity will quite often flower indoors. This is particularly true of yams, which blossom out in greenish bell-shaped flowers, individually quite small but growing in long trailing clusters that droop down gracefully among the leaves.

Although the terms "sweet potato" and "yam" have become colloquially interchangeable, the plants are two quite distinct species. To my surprise I found out the sweet potato is the real tropical one. The yam family is much bigger and more far-flung. Somehow I had expected just the opposite.

The yam belongs to the genus *Dioscorea*, which includes among its more hermitlike members one called *Dioscorea pyrenaica*, indigenous only to Europe, more specifically the Pyrenees. There it grows unmolested and uneaten, thousands of miles from any of its relatives, or, as they say in the trade, "congeners." The genus also includes *Dioscorea alata*, which produces a tuber weighing up to a hundred pounds. An excellent gourmet gift for the elephant who has everything.

The species more often found in the supermarket—possibly to avoid collapsed shopping carts—is the *Dioscorea bulbifera*, or the "air potato" yam. Although widely cultivated, from a city marketing point of view it seems to have a shyness reminiscent of its reclusive Pyrenees cousin, usually limiting its appearance to the holiday season. By the way, there's always the outside chance that a small stray *Dioscorea alata* has made its way into the batch you buy, so if your pots seem to be bulging at the seams, check the building plans of your apartment for where the structural supports are located, as you might end up with several hundred pounds of yam slumped over your windowsill.

9

Ouch! Upon the Rearing of Prickly Pears

It was with some uneasiness that I approached the planting of my first prickly pears. The thought of a massive collection of thorns on the windowsill wasn't bothering me, because I had heard the prickly pear belongs to an, oddly enough, thornless species of cactus. No, what bothered me was an old turn-of-the-century Luther Burbank flier I had found in my grand-mother's attic while hunting for an antique tulip-bulb planter I knew was up there somewhere. Stuck between the tulip-bulb planter and some ancient *National Geographics*, the flier loudly proclaimed, "A single acre of TRUE Burbank Cactus will easily carry One thousand Tons of Feed." Not to mention the fact that "The FRUIT also is produced in Enormous Quantities."

Our apartment was far from an acre in size. Still, I felt somehow an unchecked cactus growth spreading carpetlike across the room would not be fully appreciated.

My fears were not stilled by a somewhat dated bulletin from the Commonwealth Prickly Pear Board of Sydney, Australia. It seems that in 1840 a Mr. Edward Gore, who lived in Sydney, received some sample prickly pear plants from the United States. Reluctantly he parted with one of his specimens at the request of a Dr. Carlisle, of Scone, in the Upper Hunter Valley, New South Wales. Dr. Carlisle wanted to set up a cochineal industry for New South Wales. Cochineal is a red dye made from the dried female bodies of tiny scale insects that attack cacti; Dr. Carlisle planned to raise the insects on prickly pears. (The bulletin did not go on to explain what he planned to do with all the male insects.)

To make a long story short, not much more was heard of Dr. Carlisle or his cochineal, except that he was feeding the cacti to his livestock during periods of drought. Years later, however, in 1925, there were fify-eight million acres of cacti in Australia, and it was spreading at the rate of another million acres a year. All ostensibly from that one sample cactus.

In its natural desert environment the prickly pear spreads chiefly through broken-off joints carried along by seasonal streams or flash floods. Or its seeds are swallowed by birds and animals, pass undigested through their intestines, and sprout voraciously wherever they land. Since the only running water in our apartment was the gurgling plumbing, and the only birds that lived in it were Huff and Puff, two miniature parrots not about to distribute prickly pear seeds among the wild New York alleyways, I felt reasonably safe in starting a small pot. In any case, the temptation of a desert plant on the outskirts of my window jungle counterbalanced the risks involved.

Burbank described the genus *Opuntia*, to which most prickly pears belong, as the closest thing to perfection in the plant kingdom, at least from the standpoint of usefulness to people. His listing of the economic values of this "thornless wonder" is quite exhaustive:

Feed for all kinds of livestock, from chickens to cattle.

Fat young leaves (joints) delicious fried like eggplant or boiled as greens; make excellent pickles and sweetmeats; especially good with ginger and spices.

Fresh fruit; jams, jellies and preserves; red confectionery coloring.

Leaves admirably adapted for poultices, also good substitutes for hot water bottles. (Since most but not all *Opuntia* are thornless, some selectiveness would seem called for here.)

Juice used in making mucilage, also mixed with whitewash to make it weather better.

Ornamental hedges or fences.

By way of elaboration Burbank added that "the fruit and leaves are sometimes served in various other forms for food by those who are familiar with them." He didn't go into further detail on this point, but it's easy to see that one could build one's entire life around this supercactus. Not to mention the female scale insects that live on it and their red cochineal dye.

The prickly pear itself is a rather tasty fruit. However, as the name implies, eating it can be a painful experience. To avoid "prickly thumb," it is best to spear one end of the fruit with a fork and peel back the skin with a knife, much the way one peels a boiled new potato too hot to handle.

One prickly pear will supply more than enough seeds to plant. As you will soon discover, if you haven't already, it is an exceedingly seedy fruit. Try to save the seeds from the thick end of the fruit for planting. Don't ask me why, but experience—not fully scientifically controlled, I grant you—seems to indicate a higher rate of fertility at the plump end. Wash the seeds and let them dry for a day or two between newspapers or blotters.

Meanwhile, prepare the pots. The natural assumption would be that cacti and other plants native to desert or semi-desert regions do not need much nourishment. In fact, it would seem they ought to grow almost anywhere so long as they have plenty of light. This, it turns out, is far from true. Although the desert looks like a barren wasteland, its soil is actually very rich. It lacks only moisture. The Sahara was a lush paradise of green growth until nature and people between them turned off the faucets.

Prickly pear seeds, like most others, can be germinated between moist blotters or in a container lined with wet cheesecloth. Personally, because of their very diminutive and delicate early root structure, I early on took to germinating these particular seeds in the pot in which I expected them to grow. This method had one drawback: it required sterilized sand. Prickly pears, although quite hardy once beyond the seedling stage, are prone to damping off when young. The fungi that attack the tender young shoots can be carried by any soillike medium. Potting soil and humus bought packaged from a supermarket or discount store usually will be presterilized (check the label to be sure). On the other hand, sand carted home from a construction site in a shoe box most definitely will not be.

To ensure a ready supply of sterilized sand, Susan agreed to bake all dinner potatoes in the following manner: she wrapped the scrubbed potatoes in aluminum foil and laid them on a bed of sand about half an inch deep in a baking pan, and then blanketed them completely with more sand. By the time the potatoes were evenly baked and browned, the sand was sterilized and ready for either immediate use—as soon as it cooled, that is—or storage in plastic bags or coffee tins. Soil imported from the country may be prepared in the same way. Corn is very good, incidentally, roasted in sand.

I found a potting mixture of one-third sand, one-third humus, and one-third soil best for my prickly pears. The matchhead-sized seeds should be buried about a quarter of an inch below the soil. Water the soil heavily, keeping it quite moist but not muddy. It takes four to six weeks for the first shoots to surface. Sprouted in a germination tray, they're quicker about it. But what you first see emerging from the seed is the taproot, at which point you have to bury the whole thing

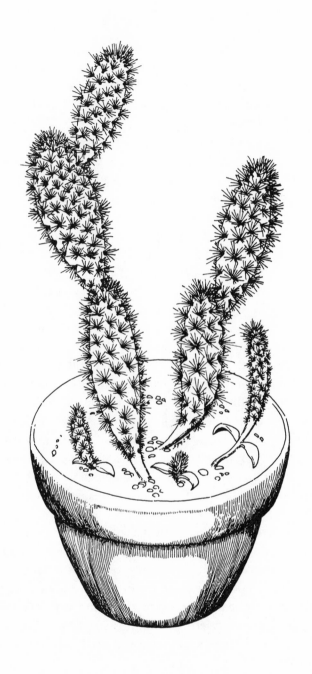

in a pot anyhow, and then it will take another two weeks or so for the first shoot to break surface. There's just no way to satisfy impatience except to start a new and different plant every week or so, ensuring that something novel will soon appear in one pot or another.

The first shoot in my prickly pear pot consisted of two tiny leaves on a stem. Although they were thick, almost fat, and obviously those of a desert plant, the leaves made it look not at all like a cactus. I began to wonder what it was we had eaten in the guise of a prickly pear.

Two weeks later I noticed a couple of very thin white hairs rising stiffly from the juncture of the two leaves. As the shoot continued to grow, a small, properly barrel-shaped cactus joint developed between the original leaves. It was covered with white hairy bristles, called "glochidia," growing out of tiny holes, or "areoles," spaced evenly all over the cactus.

This was my first indication that the "thornless wonder" isn't exactly bald. Granted it didn't have full-fledged thorns, but the bristles were still far from comfortable when they got stuck in my thumb. Prickly pears must be handled with care because the glochidia have microscopic barbs at their tips, making it a lot harder for them to get out of a thumb than in.

The prickly pear quite often sends out double shoots from each seed. I don't know why this happens; maybe it's a sort of double indemnity program to ensure propagation in the hostile desert. Whatever the case, one shoot is always noticeably larger, stronger, and more robust than the other, and in a few months the dominant one has usually taken over completely and the weaker expired. The professional grower would probably advise removing the smaller of the two almost at once, since it serves only to drain energy from the main plant. With a soft spot for the underdog, I tended to let them both grow. But when I did remove the extra sprout, I had to admit the growth was demonstrably better.

Being desert plants, *Opuntia* need a great deal of sun and are best grown in windows with southern or western exposure. Surprisingly, they also need a fair amount of water. This is not to say you can't leave the plant without water for quite some time, when going on vacation, for instance; it might be somewhat shriveled on your return, but will regain its sturdy composure in a short period with good watering. On the other hand, under normal circumstances it should be watered with the same regularity as, though in lesser amount than, your other plants. By the same token, it should be fertilized as richly as any other plant.

When the *Opuntia* really show their heritage is from October to January. During this "resting period," as it is known, especially if you are trying to induce it to flower, or "forcing" it, the plant should be given no fertilizer and watered very sparingly, or even not at all, for a month, beginning around November.

Presented with these suddenly not too prosperous conditions, it's as if the plant feels its time has come. If it's going to keep up the lineage, it had better reproduce quickly. Hence the flowers, which in turn become fruit with seeds. Seeds can survive conditions a plant cannot. Lying dormant through the lean years, they will germinate when conditions become more favorable.

Grown indoors, the prickly pear will rarely flower the second or third year. However, the fourth year you stand a good chance of seeing some very attractive yellow flowers. If you don't manage to get blossoms the fourth year, you still have an interesting plant and the fifth year to look forward to. And at least it's not one of those rare orchids that take thirty years to bloom.

10

Artichokes, Sí! Artichokes, No!

Since both Susan and I are very fond of artichokes, it was to
be expected that sooner or later I would try my luck with them.
I had an instinctive feeling the attempt wouldn't work, however. So before wasting a whole artichoke trying to figure out
which, if any, part of it might produce a new plant, I decided
to do a little spadework at the library.

There seemed not to be an extensive literature available on
the artichoke. I came away with the scant information that it
was thistlelike in appearance, originated around the Mediterranean, and had been under cultivation since ancient times.

Apparently the Artichoke Consumer Association had
switched public relations agencies somewhere along the pas-
sage of history. Early in the game it was the young leaves,
blanched or au naturel, that were eaten. Today it's the fleshy
base of the immature flowerhead we relish.

There it was in black and white. All along we'd been eating
immature flowers—obviously not a chance of propagation. No
seed, and not enough plant to it to offer the remotest possibility
of taking root if stuck into the earth. Nothing!

I thought no more of growing artichokes till the following
spring. Then one day, passing the greengrocer's, I spotted a
bushel basket lined with newspaper and filled with singularly

ugly gnarled tubers. JERUSALEM ARTICHOKES 49¢ A POUND, the sign above them informed me in a crayon scrawl.

That seemed reasonable enough. From what I had learned, artichokes were extensively cultivated around there. But what had happened to these? They looked like potatoes with lumps on them.

Closer inspection showed that every lump had in its center a smaller lump and, in some cases, this second lump appeared to be opening up into tiny purple potential leaves. The whole bud was not much bigger than a broken pencil point. Still, it was obvious the Jerusalem artichokes would sprout. Maybe they were just like potato tubers. I bought two pounds, one for planting and one for eating.

While Susan dug up a recipe for them, I tried to find out what we were about to eat. The first thing I discovered was that the Jerusalem artichoke neither is an artichoke nor does it come from Jerusalem. It is native to North America, and was first chronicled by Champlain during his second voyage (1604–07). He observed the native inhabitants in of Nanset Harbor, Massachusetts, cultivating the edible tubers. In what was probably the first botanical account of the Jerusalem artichoke, Parkinson in his *Paradisus* (1629) listed it under the name *Batatas de Canada*, or "Canadian potato." This was in opposition to the "Virginia potato," or potato as we know it. However, the term didn't take.

The "artichoke" half of the tuber's name is derived from its flavor. Peeled, boiled, and served with a white sauce, or gently sautéed, it does taste very like an artichoke, though the texture is firmer than that of the true artichoke, and somewhat woody as compared with its namesake's buttery consistency.

As to its Christian name, as it were, Thomas Love Peacock sheds some light on its derivation with his observations on the Anglo-Saxon genius for modifying names to make them more

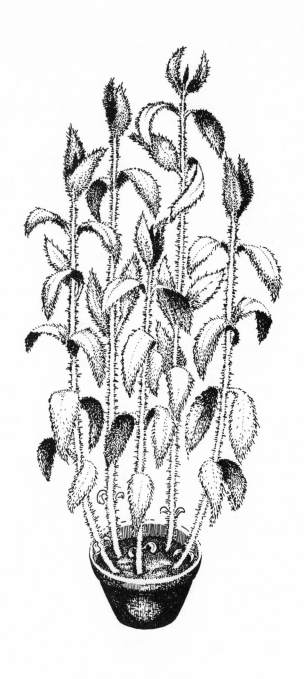

palatable to its own tongue. Writing in 1861, he commented: "We have an excellent old vegetable, the artichoke of which we eat the head; we have another of subsequent introduction, of which we eat the root, and which we also call artichoke. . . . This last is a species of *helianthus* or sunflower. . . . It is therefore a girasole, or turn-to-the-sun. From the girasole we have made Jerusalem and from the Jerusalem artichoke we make Palestine soup."

Although there is some debate over the correctness of this derivation, it is the one most often proffered. Those who say it's not so offer no alternative explanation. In any case, what I wanted to do was plant my Jerusalem artichokes speedily, not study the finer points of name derivation. Particularly since I found that not only were the sprouts already growing, indeed very much like potatoes, but also the thin, apparently sensitive skin of the tubers was beginning to shrivel.

The land around Cape Cod, where Jerusalem artichokes were cultivated by Native Americans, has always conjured to my mind an extensive stretch of sand and dunes. Therefore I perched my Jerusalem artichokes in a mixture of three-fourths sand and one-fourth humus. The plants grew rapidly from the half-exposed tubers. At one point, when the most luxuriant plant was about six inches tall, I put a ruler into the soil and proudly marked its height. Coming back about five hours later, I was amazed to see that the plant had shot up almost half an inch during my absence. I've since read claims of this plant reaching a height of ten or twelve feet.

Before I had worried long about the inadequacy of our nine-foot ceilings to the situation, however, the plants began to die. There had been two basic flaws in my original reasoning. For one, I had assumed, since the tubers were already beginning to sprout, I could get away with burying them only partially, so I could watch them grow sooner. Unfortunately, although the sprouts were beginning to shoot up vigorously by the end of the third day, the sensitive tubers, exposed to city air and its pollutants, began to decay. Rot took over the plant, and that was that. The tuber should be covered in planting with approximately two inches of soil.

My second blunder was the assumption that Jerusalem artichokes would thrive in a mixture composed mainly of sand. To the contrary, they like a very rich mixture. I learned to use almost half soil and half humus, with maybe an additional 10 percent sand to keep it loose.

I also learned to use an oversized pot, since this plant does grow so rapidly; it soon becomes "pot-bound" in what starts out as a pot fully proportionate to its size. I found it a good practice not to repot the Jerusalem artichoke during the year. Part of the fun in growing the tuber lies in watching its extravagant growth, and repotting, with time out for the plant to adjust to its new surroundings, interrupts the growth process.

A bit of incidental information for dieters: the tuber of the Jerusalem artichoke so far contains no starch and only about 2 percent free sugar. A group of Swedish botanists set out to try to boost the sugar content by crossing the Jerusalem artichoke with the sunflower—this is in order to facilitate using the tuber as a source of sugar much like the sugar beet. I've never heard any reports of their success, but if ever the Jerusalem artichoke did manage to become sweeter, I suppose we'd have the Swede Jerusalem, which would present future etymologists with considerable food for thought.

When Jerusalem artichokes are young, in their first and second years of growth, they nestle well on the windowsill with the other plants. By the time they reach five or six feet, the older leaves towards the bottom have shriveled and died, so the floor may be the best place for the pots. The stems add a foresty air to the otherwise empty space below, and the tops are given a few more feet to stretch in the sun. As the lower leaves die they can be pinched off and allowed to lie on the soil in the pot.

If not perhaps the most orderly way to dispose of them, I found it functional. The leaves decay slowly, making a good rich mulch, and at the same time the layer keeps moisture from escaping the soil too readily.

Moisture is most important for Jerusalem artichokes. The stems of these plants have a disproportionately high water content compared to others, such as mangoes or avocados, with woody trunks. The Jerusalem artichoke will wilt quickly if deprived of water. Once the soil has been allowed to dry out, the top growth will droop over completely within a day.

In spite of this vulnerability, its recuperative powers, provided the wilting has not progressed too far, are amazing. One weekend when we had gone away and I had neglected to water the plants before leaving, we returned to find the Jerusalem artichokes bent over almost double from thirst. Lo and behold, three hours after a good soaking they were upright and unscathed. I could almost hear the water being slurped up and the tops recovering, so quick was the rejuvenation.

These fuzzy perennials will die down in the late fall. In some cases, even indoors, they will flower before doing so, bearing large purplish discs three inches or more across. Mine never obliged; they didn't get enough sunlight in our north windows. But there is no need to throw away a wilted Jerusalem artichoke. If it has completed a successful growing cycle, there will be a fresh clump of new tubers beside the old one and, come spring, they will sprout.

Meanwhile, you can hide the pot away in any cool dark spot, but don't water it. Once winter has departed, try to locate your old, dried pot of Jerusalem artichokes, water them well and put them in the sunniest spot in your window. A sunny balcony or fire escape would be an even better place for them—except the neighbors above you might take to trimming the tops off to keep their view unobstructed.

I I

The Russian Mammoth from Kansas

Everybody's got to get into the act. Our two miniature parrots, Huff and Puff, were not to be excluded. Being rather exuberant eaters, they scattered seeds about not only in their cage, but several feet outside it as well. I sometimes suspected them of deliberately aiming for my windowsill. Assorted odd, but small and manageable grasses sprouted in the pots closest to their cage. They seemed to make good ground cover, and on dying down made a little extra mulch for the plants I was growing, so I didn't mind the parrots' assistance.

Things began to get out of hand, however. Several sunflower seeds had sprouted in one pot—and did they grow! The original inhabitant, a struggling young litchi, was being completely crowded out. Checking back to the invaluable library at the New York Botanical Gardens for information on this upstart, I found that the sunflower itself doesn't like crowding. My plants, although growing rapidly, were definitely stunted, at least by the standards of the U.S. Department of Agriculture, Division of Chemistry, Bulletin Number 60, which described the sunflower as an annual with a rather stout, erect herbaceous stem one to three inches in diameter and five to twenty feet high. Had my name been Jack, I could have seen a beanstalk in my future. As it was, my plants were barely a foot high after a month.

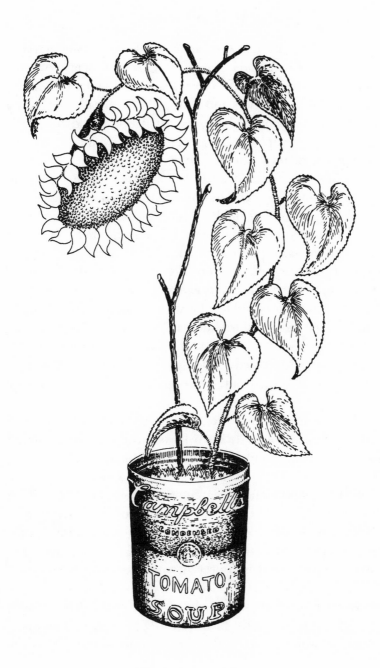

Part of the problem was, as the sunflower's name implies, sun. Or, more accurately, lack of it. Our apartment wasn't exactly the equivalent of the Great Plains, the sunflower's native land, as far as openness and light go. The so-called terrace, a fire escape in poor disguise, looked like it would be a little healthier for the plants. I transferred some to individual pots and put them at the sunniest edge.

I still wasn't fully satisfied. A twenty-foot sunflower would be something to match, and my transplanted ones might not catch up. When Huff and Puff weren't looking, I swiped a couple of super-duper sunflower seeds from them. These I planted, to boost their morale, in a spacious old pretzel tin of indeterminate age disguised by pop art as a Campbell's tomato soup can at some point in its career. I punched some drainage holes in the bottom and filled it with two-thirds soil dug up in the country and one-third humus. It would have taken a dozen or more three-dollar bags of potting soil to fill the pretzel can, and the expense seemed a little high even for a twenty-foot sunflower. As it turned out, however, this poorer soil mixture didn't bother the sunflowers a bit.

Apparently the sunflower, at least in diminutive form, will grow almost anyplace. In many parts of the Midwest it is found primarily around railroad sidings and dumps where nothing else grows. This is not due to any inherent patriotic urge to beautify America, however. Sunflowers are loners, disliking competition. Should you grow yours on a balcony, or near birds, where stray seeds may be deposited, make sure to weed out all extraneous plants as they appear. Even two or three relatively small ones could prevent your sunflower from developing to its full size.

Once removed to the balcony, my sunflowers thrived, though I had to gently brush off a light crust of soot every week. Up, up, and away, their height proportionate to the size of their pots. The one in the pretzel can was pushing seven feet.

They blossomed too, again in sizes proportionate to the pots. The larger the pot, the larger the flower. I should say flowers. Although I managed to cultivate only one large flowerhead per plant, I discovered this flower wasn't a flower at all. It was a natural bouquet. The sunflower is a compound flower. Just as the eye of a dragonfly is composed of a number of "eyes" bunched together, so each sunflower is actually several dozen simple blossoms growing together on a disc, each one producing a seed.

As the sunflowers followed the sun day after day—they literally turn almost a full hundred and eighty degrees each day to get every last ray of sun directly in their faces—I waited anxiously for the seeds to develop. Huff and Puff would be reimbursed with fresh, wholesome, homegrown sunflower seeds.

The rest of them I would eat myself. My blooming sunflowers had reminded me of how those of us assigned to the back rows in grade school used to buy little two-cent packets of Indian Head Sunflower Seeds from the corner candy store to eat while the teacher carefully drilled us on the spelling of "obfuscation," bound to be in the next spelling bee.

I remember sitting there looking out the window, dreaming of riding my stallion across the sunflower-filled plains of eastern Europe, where, I'd learned from the encyclopedia, the flower is extensively cultivated for its fine cooking oil.

What had started me on a sunflower seed binge in earnest in those early school days was Tolstoy's *The Cossack*. Everybody in his wild and heroic Caucasus wanderings was constantly munching sunflower seeds. I worked very hard at the Russian technique, which involved feeding the mouth with a steady supply of seeds, splitting them in one side of the mouth, separating seed from hull with the tongue, and all the while expelling an equally steady stream of empty shells from the other side of the mouth. Although I got up a fairly decent speed (outside the classroom), I never did manage the machine-gun-fire rapidity with which I mentally endowed cossack soldiers. One czar of Russia allegedly gave his soldiers two and a half pounds of the highly nutritious seeds a day, which I had no doubt made them the strong silent type.

A further stimulus to the sunflower-seed cult when I was a kid was the Shoshones. Not only did they eat sunflower seeds, they used to extract a purple war paint from the shells as well. In our Cowboys-and-Indians games there was never a dearth of Indians. After all, they had to leave a trail of sunflower-seed shells behind.

Another group of avid sunflower-seed eaters, I later learned, are the Chinese. They eat them as we do salted nuts and between courses of a meal.

Where sunflower seeds are not so enthusiastically consumed, I hear, is in Kansas, where they originally came from. Even the fact that the sunflower is the Kansas state flower doesn't seem to enhance their status. Presumably this is because, although it is a native American flower, the variety most commonly grown is the one producing the big striped seed known as the Russian Mammoth—decidedly foreign.

Whatever the case, I intended to eat mine. September came. The flowers were in full bloom, and I continued to water the pots heavily to ensure plants of maximum size. The sunflower, being herbaceous like its relative, the Jerusalem artichoke, needs plenty of moisture. Unfortunately, even with the summer's careful tending, I didn't get to reap my crop that year. We went on vacation, and on our return I found the sunflower seeds thoroughly harvested by the local winged inhabitants. The few plants kept indoors had never flowered. I was left empty-handed till the following summer.

Should you get yours to the harvesting stage, however, do check with your local police department before going around munching the seeds in public places. In Endicott, Washington, there's a law, unless recently revoked, against eating sunflower seeds on the streets or in business establishments.

12

Ponderings on the Pithy Pomegranate

The pomegranate made its annual appearance in our neighborhood markets in late fall to early winter. I suppose that's why it was associated in my mind with Christmas and the holiday season. I say associated because, for no particular reason really, except perhaps that there was always so much else to eat at that time of year, I had never gotten around to trying one—or so I thought.

Well, I was mistaken on both counts. The pomegranate is decidedly not a lover of the winter solstice. On the contrary, the hotter the summer, the better. It's a semidesert, very drought-resistant shrub, originating in Iran but now widespread in the warmer, drier areas of the world. As to never having partaken of pomegranate, little did I realize that the grenadine syrup Susan used in desserts was made from pomegranate juice.

Having found out that the pomegranate's favorite abode is the southwest tip of Saudi Arabia, around Aden, I questioned the advisability of growing the bush at home. After all, one must draw the line somewhere. Keeping the apartment close to a hundred and twenty degrees all day seemed a bit excessive. Still, even if it didn't give its all, maybe the pomegranate bush would at least consent to sprout under our apartment's far from favorable conditions. It was worth a try.

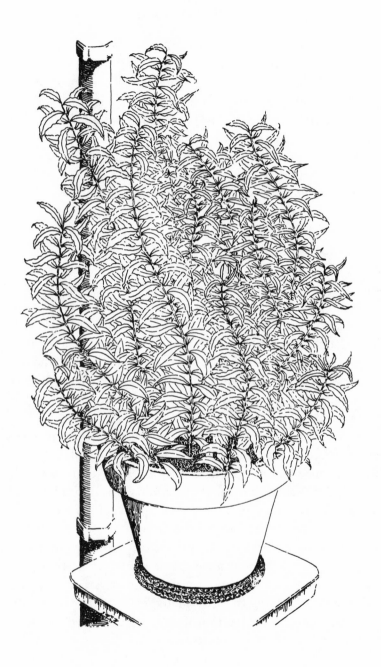

I waited till the end of December to buy pomegranates. During most of the winter there was a total lack of direct sunlight reaching our apartment. Hopefully, I reasoned, by the time the seeds germinated, a little early spring sun would be creeping high enough over the building across the alley to sneak a ray or two into our window.

Struggling with my first, supposedly edible pomegranate, I could see where the name *pomme grenate*, or seedy apple, given it in the Middle Ages, was more than appropriate. I could also see that it must be the greatest thing in the world for kids. My shirt and handkerchief were both liberally splattered with bright red juice by the time I had cut through it.

My first approach to the fruity insides was to try to separate the slippery seed coverings, or "arils," from the seeds themselves. I gave that up almost immediately as hopeless. In Syria pomegranates are served stewed with sugar and sprinkled with rose water. But apparently, to judge from the kitchen shelves, rose water was something we didn't keep around with the regularity of vanilla. The best I could come up with along this line at the moment was Susan's Chanel, and it didn't seem a fitting substitute.

Since grenadine syrup is made by crushing the arils, seeds and all, I concluded that the seeds, if not an integral part of the pomegranate's taste, must be at least edible. With fruits you've never eaten before, it is wise to ascertain at the beginning what is edible and what is not; some seeds, peach pits, for instance, are poisonous if eaten in large quantities.

Munching the arils, seeds and all, turned out to be a functional, if not the tastiest, form of nutrition. More satisfactory, from both the gourmet and the after-dinner gardening points of view, was sucking the arils off and ejecting the seeds. I deposited them on an old section of newspaper on top of the bookshelf to dry for a couple of days.

Actually this discussion is putting the seed before the fruit, or the garden before the dinner. The first problem for the consumer is really how most judiciously to expose the pomegranate's contents. Cutting it in half, of course, displays the inside well. That's how I proceeded to get the only red polka-dotted shirt in the neighborhood. Peeling it like an orange is guaranteed to paint your arms with sticky juice up to the elbows, and even if you feel no affinity to Lady Macbeth it will take a lot of washing to remove.

After three pomegranates and six showers I knew the makeup of the pomegranate well enough to devise what I consider the most foolproof system for breaking and entering. Grasp the pomegranate firmly, preferably with the stem end facing you. Then chop off a deep disc from the other, calyx end. The calyx end is the one with the brown tuft, all that remains to show where the shriveled flower petals fell off. Once a disc has been cut out of a pomegranate, you can peel back the crisp outer skin and divide the fruit into its natural segments without its squirting too much.

Conquering the technique of eating a pomegranate and extricating the devious seeds is the biggest hurdle the home seed gatherer faces. The rest of the after-dinner ritual is easy by comparison. With the pomegranate I reverted to germinating the seeds in individual closed containers lined on the bottom with moist cheesecloth. Any small, clean jar with a lid, like sample-sized jam jars or the plastic ounce-sized candied fruit jars found on grocery shelves around fruitcake and plum pudding season, is ideal for them.

An occasional by-product of this method is mold on the seeds, but it doesn't seem to really impede germination. In fact, since I've had better success germinating the seeds this way than planting them directly in the pot, the mold may even perform some positive botanical function of which I'm unaware. I probably never would have gotten my first papayas growing had it not been for a little unsolicited assistance from some unknown mold . . . but more on that later.

As soon as the pomegranate seeds have cracked open, usually in from four to six weeks, and the short white taproot has poked out slightly, the seeds can be transferred to a pot filled with a mixture of about two-thirds potting soil and one-third humus, with an additional 10 percent sand. It is particularly important to transfer the seed as soon as it has begun growing if your germination container has a case of mold. While mold and an uncracked seed seem to live together happily enough, an emerging root hasn't the same tough independence and may be destroyed by its companion. To lessen the chances of mold damage, rinse the sprouting seed carefully under slowly running tepid water before planting it.

Poke a hole in the waiting soil with a pencil point, to a depth of about a quarter of an inch. Put the seed in, root down the way it belongs, cover over lightly with soil, and water it enough so the soil fills in around the seed. It will be another two weeks or so before the plant itself surfaces, its seed leaves twirled together in an unusual, flowerlike knot.

In its natural habitat the pomegranate grows to a large bush or small tree. In our apartment it never grew to more than a low shrub. Without the sun it just didn't try very hard. However, I've heard of its even blooming indoors after a few years, bearing pretty red and pinkish flowers, given plenty of light and good fertilization.

There are two things to remember if you are trying to encourage it to flower. Though basically a semidesert plant, the pomegranate needs a rich soil, so fertilize it well. Secondly, though most of your other tropical plants enjoy a dewy atmosphere, the pomegranate likes it dry. So avoid getting water on its leaves and keep it in a place away from your other plants, which by their collective moist pots will keep the humidity high in their vicinity.

If you haven't a spot sunny enough to permit the plant to bloom, the pomegranate still has the advantage of growing where some other plants won't. The top of a covered radiator near the window usually makes an excellent site, as does any other well-lit nook wanting a touch of greenery but too dry or hot for your other plants. Just water the pot a little more, to compensate for the high evaporation rate incurred by keeping it in a hot spot. Also, though the plant top prefers a dry atmosphere, its roots will die without moisture in the soil. I learned to keep the soil almost as wet as in my other pots, only cutting down the watering for a month each year to produce an artificial drought, in the hope of forcing a bloom.

I was never lucky enough to get any flower action. But if you do, you might as well go a step further and try to raise your own, if probably diminutive, pomegranates. For this, unless you're in the habit of keeping a hive of bees in the kitchen for honey, you'll probably have to fertilize the flowers yourself. I once contemplated putting a beehive outside the window. But instead, to fertilize the pepper plants I got to flower, I used a cotton swab on a toothpick, poking it gently into one flower after the other to transfer the pollen. It might not buzz, but it works. And if I got tiny peppers that way, it should work for tiny pomegranates as well.

Having given up hope of getting the pomegranates to flower, I took to planting more to a pot than before, for, in the only nook left for it at the outskirts of my jungle, the bush tended to grow straight up in sprigs instead of branching. It blissfully ignored most of my dogged attempts at pruning, in most cases simply sending up a new leading stem rather than spreading out. So I began planting half a dozen or even a dozen to an eight-inch pot. This meant fertilizing the lot quite heavily. But the density of the stand compensated for the singleness of the stalks, and as a "multiple bush" it did very nicely in "greening up" the corner where nothing grew but a hot-water pipe.

13

"How Come There Are Grape Leaves on Your Papaya Plant?"

Two months after the first prim and proper-looking shoots came up in the pot carefully labeled PAPAYA, the plants reached the gawky stage. Gangly and long-stemmed, they just looked too tall for their leaves. It was autumn, and our northern window no longer coaxed in the lazy sun. They're stretching for light, I thought, poor things. I propped them up with a chopstick. After waiting six months for those shoots, I was taking every precaution against illness and injury.

Another month passed. Thoughtfully I added another chopstick on top. Straight on up they grew. Soon they were three Scotch-taped chopsticks high, and the leaves were no bigger. I remained undaunted.

The papaya, though tree-sized at maturity, is not a tree but a large perennial herb. It doesn't branch off the way trees usually do, but more closely resembles the banana in its growing pattern, except that it grows taller and the crown from which the leaves sprout rises with the tip of the plant. Since the new leaves, even if nowhere near the size I had expected to see by now, were green at the crown and healthy, I was confident if I could only keep the plants struggling along through the winter, they would fill out in the first warmth and sunshine of spring.

I hadn't counted on Susan's observant eye. Returning to the apartment from a Sunday afternoon in the country, she strode purposefully over to the papaya pot and inspected it closely. Then she turned with an impish grin.

"How come there are grape leaves on your papaya plant?" she asked.

Actually, every house should have a grapevine or two by a window. They climb quickly and gracefully, and can be trained to edge the window frame with a green leafy border. Granted, my temperate grapevines were a little out of place in the window jungle. But that had bothered neither them nor me until I'd found out they were interlopers. Somehow the window would no longer have seemed complete without their long brown vines. After all, one can't swing Tarzan-style from here to there without a proper liana looping around among the mangoes and avocados.

They were already growing, poor helpless clinging vines doing no one but the stooping Scotch-taped chopsticks any harm. I couldn't bring myself to wantonly throw them out. Besides, they might bear grapes.

The grapevine is one of the most widespread of fruit bearers in the temperate zones. Even before people crossed the ocean, in either direction, it was growing in profusion in both Europe and North America. That's a safe bet without going into the debate over which Europeans actually "discovered" America— something I'd rather not get involved in here since, being Scandinavian, I'd have to opt for Leif Eriksson, and this chapter would grow all out of bounds. Whoever it was—Columbus, Eriksson, or anybody else—the grapevine, although a different species than that in Europe, was here, too, when they arrived, maybe even under cultivation.

In excavations of Swiss villages dating from the Bronze Age, grape seeds have been found under circumstances implying cultivation. Grape and wine production records were kept in hieroglyphics as early as the fourth century, Egyptian time (2400 B.C.). It would appear that both of these ancient vineyard

regions cultivated a grape of excellent taste, the *Vitis vinifera*, originating around the Caspian Sea. The consensus still has it the best grape of all, particularly for wine production, even in today's age of improved hybrids.

The *V. vinifera* being the superior species, American grape growers naturally wanted to cultivate this European variety at home, so they imported vast quantities from France. A native American plant louse, the phylloxera, however, did not see eye to eye with the growers and promptly destroyed all the *V. vinifera*. Then to add insult to injury, the louse shipped out and just as promptly destroyed all the grapevines in Europe. At which point the American growers ended up shipping their native vines over to Europe. The American species, over no doubt long years of struggle, had developed an immunity to the harassment of this pest.

So when you come right down to it, that "imported" European grape is just coming home. Only, of course, the varying environment of sun, rain, and soil in different parts of Europe does put a different stamp on American vines living there. Besides which, European growers were not to be consoled with American grapes. They grafted what they could salvage of their own stock onto the disease-resistant American roots. To be really accurate about it, then, you'd have to say that what they've got now is a European grape with American roots.

But none of this need trouble the owner of the homegrown grapevine. I never had any lice on my vines. And, given a window to wander up, they adapt themselves to a wide variety of soil conditions, even accidental ones.

My first grapevines sprouted from errant seeds. The window cleaner knocked over an open jar in which I had been drying some seeds. They were waiting their turn for planting; at the moment there was no vacancy on the ledge. Susan picked up most of them with the vacuum cleaner, and I scooped the rest off the sill into my hands. Nevertheless, they were small, and a number of them had scattered into assorted pots. By the time Susan pointed out that there were in fact incipient grapevines and not papayas in the papaya pot, they had sprouted among the mangoes and pineapples, too.

So it seems almost any soil will do for grapes. Although fertilizer should be added to poor soil, with grapes there's no worry about its being too loamy, too sandy, or too clayish. The plants will keep growing anyway. For the biggest and best plants, however, I used two-thirds potting soil to one-third humus.

Digging out my first grapevines carefully from the pots they had strayed into, I put them all in with the ersatz papaya. The idea was that the soil mixture for the papaya—which seemingly was not going to put in an appearance, in that pot at any rate—had been made up particularly rich and so with regular fertilization could support a number of vines. Indeed it did.

Not at all sure I would arrive at a full gourmet's selection of grape clusters starting out this way, I later started a pot sown with more precision, scattering maybe a dozen seeds from different types of grapes, blue, red, and green, and covering them with about an eighth-inch of humus. Having gone in for grapes, I might as well select, not settle. The various vines would climb up different ways, maybe. They'd certainly have differently shaped leaves and tend to drop their leaves at different times, thus giving an all-around lushness to our window border.

A mature grapevine thrives on sun, preferring long, dry, warm to hot summers. But while a window with direct sunlight will produce the most luxuriant vines, I managed to get eight- to ten-foot vines in two years in a north window. A young vine, as opposed to its older sibling, should not be exposed to more than two hours of direct sunlight a day; it might get sunburned.

Once a vinery group is six inches or so tall, add another

quarter-inch of humus to the pot. Also cover the soil with any extra fallen leaves you might have around.

Give young grapes a stake to climb. This is essential. Grapevines grow faster if they can climb up. When there is nothing for their tendrils to grasp, the vines droop over and run along the ground, always trying to reach up. If after growing horizontally for a while they still fail to find something to latch onto, to lift themselves, they will simply give up and stop growing.

Susan gave our vines green yarn to grow up one Christmas. It made an excellent ladder strung crisscross at the side of our bay window. I tried to guide the vines up diagonally, rather than letting them grow straight up. They can be coaxed this way, but for some strange reason they balk absolutely at twining downward. They simply won't grow upside down, although turning them topsy-turvy sometimes will make them send out new shoots farther down the main vine, producing a thicker, more lush border. More usually, however, they stop growing altogether until the following season.

Many tropical plants have a resting period, when there is no noticeable growth; it is brief, usually lasting only a month or so. Temperate-zone plants like the grape, on the other hand, may rest as long as five months. Once fall comes, the changes outdoors are noticeable enough to the house grapevine to make it have thoughts of reverting to nature. Grown indoors, the grapevine often remains green year-round, but sometimes it will stop growing come winter.

If the leaves change color and wither, it is an easy matter to trim the plant down and keep it in hibernation till spring. Besides, they usually turn more slowly indoors, adding a colorful speckled red foliage to a window jungle late into autumn.

For maximum growth the next year the vines should be cut back whether the leaves turn or not. In the case of the grape don't be afraid to do a lot of cutting. Take off as much as 80 percent, leaving only ten to twelve inches aboveground. While it is hibernating, water the plant as usual or perhaps just a bit less.

Left to my own devices, and having acquired by laissez-faire means several handsome nine-foot vines without cutting back, I would tend to let things be. For while pruning might make grapevines grow faster *next* year, without cutting back they overgrow the window *this* year. Which is why, I suppose, one year for my birthday Susan gave me a small machete. There were no instructions, but I took the hint and pruned the plants a bit.

14

The Secret of the Golden Papaya

It was purely by accident that I discovered the secret of a successful papaya patch. When I brought home my first plump tropical "melon," I was confident these were going to be some of my more obliging seeds. The papaya is reputed to be one of the easiest of all tropical plants to grow. Each fruit contains hundreds of seeds. Supposedly they're so impatient to sprout, they have been known to begin sending roots out when the fruit is still ripening. Furthermore, a papaya under good growing conditions reaches the bearing stage as soon as nine months after it first sprouts. With several fruits on a papaya plant, and several hundred seeds in each fruit, I could see a papaya population explosion was imminent. I cleared a large portion of the table by the window.

Many, many papaya desserts later, not only had I not found a papaya with seeds already germinating, but all I had in the papaya patch was a couple of empty pots and three little see-through containers filled with moist cheesecloth, papaya seeds, and mold. Lots of mold. Susan several times encouraged me to dispose of the display. But I held out stubbornly for my laissez-faire gardening philosophy and let the seeds mold on their merry way. Sure enough, three months later the seeds had sprouted—thanks to the same unpopular mold.

A blanket of mold is not really essential to papaya propagation. But it was a clue to the real secret. I found the explanation of what had happened under the blanket in the fine print of a footnote on page 592 of *Tropical and Subtropical Agriculture*, by Ochse, Soule, Dijkman, and Wehlburg: "The aril around each seed must be removed before it can be planted or dried for storage."

So that was it. Papaya seeds come wrapped in their own little natural "baggies," like pomegranate seeds. However, unlike pomegranate arils, which one eats, papaya arils, almost invisible, go unnoticed by the gourmet. As a papaya seed dries, the thin Jell-O-like coating dries with it, protecting the seed from moisture and effectively preventing germination. In the case of my seeds, apparently, the mold had managed after three months to undermine this shell, letting moisture in and activating the germination process.

The same footnote explained that the usual method of removing the aril is to "rub a number of seeds together on a fine-meshed screen under running water. After they have been thoroughly dried, seeds will remain viable for several years if put into airtight containers." Privately I thought this the long way round the papaya bush, since the seeds came packed in their own airtight containers to begin with.

I suppose the aril keeps a seed from germinating until the season with conditions most suitable for seedlings rolls around again. And I will concede that without the inhibitions of their arils, papayas might overrun somebody's country or other. But I was thankful to be so unexpectedly rid of mine.

This hurdle over, presumably I'd have no more problems with papaya plants. You will recall that, though as big as a full-grown tree and somewhat like a palm in build, the papaya is neither, but an arborescent herb. This ought to mean it looks like a tree and grows like an herb, that is, withers to the ground each year. But the papaya doesn't wither to the ground; it keeps growing and bearing for years on end. So it doesn't fit the dictionary definition of an herb, either. I've given up and now refer to it simply as a plant. That should be safe enough.

One warning to potential papaya growers I should note here. The papaya plant is probably the most sensitive of all tropical fruit bearers to standing water and poor aeration. For this reason the standard porous terra-cotta pot is a must for them. Likewise, the drainage hole must be covered with larger-than-normal stoppers, preferably pieces of broken pottery two inches or so across. The papaya's sensitive roots will die off after as short a time as forty-eight hours in standing water. A loose soil mixture, half humus, half potting soil, with a good handful of vermiculite, best prevents caking and throttling of the delicate roots. Their frailty also makes the papaya seedlings somewhat wary of transplanting, so I soon adopted the practice of planting the seeds in pots larger than I would normally use for seedlings, eight inches or more in diameter.

With my new footnote instructions on undressing papaya seeds, I set to work on a fresh dessert-destined "melon." I spooned a heap of the moist, somewhat messy seeds onto a newspaper. Experimentation soon showed that you don't really have to scrub the seeds against a screen to remove the arils. Squeezing them slightly off-center made the seed pop out of the aril. The technique is similar to the children's practice of squeezing watermelon seeds between their fingers to shoot them at unsuspecting targets.

In fact, it's a little too similar. Demonstrating the process to Susan, I turned to get another piece of paper on which to rest the de-ariled seeds. There was a soft splat on the back of my neck, then another. A third seed sailed narrowly past my ear. Paying no attention, since Susan was putting on the wide-eyed innocent act, I returned to the table and selected the juiciest seed I could find. . . .

An hour later, picking up stray papaya seeds from the four corners of the room, I had a respectable pile of the little black

wrinkled balls lying in a warm spot to dry. The next day I placed a dozen seeds on the soil of the waiting pots and covered them with a quarter-inch of straight humus. They looked fine.

Five weeks later plants broke the surface, not the full dozen I had planted, but seven at least. When they developed to a height of about two inches, I got ready for the painful necessity of pulling out all the weaker ones so the remaining plant would have free rein of the pot without having to fight for it. I tried to lift out the plants with my trusty old nail file and transfer them to new pots as gently as I could.

A few survived the journey, but most of the plants lasted only a couple of days in their new quarters. The papaya roots were registering their objection to being relocated without taking the whole pot of homestead dirt with them.

This was still only the beginning of my papaya problems. One day I woke up to find that every last one of the surviving plants had toppled over. Even a mature papaya root structure is fairly weak, and plants frequently tip over in tropical winds. But mine weren't tall enough to be affected by any winds. Not to mention the fact that, although our apartment had seen many strange visitors, including the perennial New York burglar, we hadn't yet been hosts to a hurricane. Poring over the plants, I noticed that close to ground level their stems were a little pinched and drawn-looking. I propped them up with toothpicks.

But my worst fears were confirmed the next day. The pinching was even more pronounced. No doubt about it, they were infected with damping off, the bane of every plantation manager. As a fungus thriving in moist atmosphere, it is always a particularly painful topic to the grower of jungle crops.

I have ransacked libraries, garden centers, and hospitals for a cure to damping off—all without success. There are some chemicals on the market that claim to retard its growth, but this particular class of fungi, though microscopic in size, spreads so quickly the only real remedy is to dispose of the plant, lock, stock, and pot. Saving the soil for new plants is like sticking a child with measles in a hospital ward because there's no room anywhere else. When it's really putting its best foot forward, the fungus can spread and infect a plant sitting next door to the originally diseased one in less than a day. While it normally does not attack mature plants, it will lie in wait with everlasting patience for the next batch of seedlings to come along.

Having disposed of the contaminated papaya pots, I started all over again, this time using the moist cheesecloth-lined container method. There was a remarkable variation in germination time. Those seeds sprouting, about 75 percent of the total, took anywhere from one to six weeks. As soon as a few cracked open and the pale taproot stretched out, I transferred them to a pot poked full of holes about a quarter-inch deep with a pencil.

This batch fared better, but now I had new problems. The grown papaya likes sunshine. Its seedlings do not. I learned this lesson the hard way. Until the plants are three inches tall or so, they should have no more than about an hour of direct sunlight a day. After that the more the merrier, provided the soil is kept moist (but not wet).

Having another batch of papaya seedlings destroyed, this time apparently by too much sun, I began to wonder gloomily how many more unknown problems lay ahead, and how many of the fruits we would end up eating before I got a good papaya patch going. I decided I'd better check into other possible uses of the fruit besides simple consumption. That's when I found out I'd not only been devouring papayas in various forms all my life, but I'd probably been brushing my teeth with them as well.

The most widespread use of the papaya is not in the form of the fruit itself, though in the tropics it is one of the most common and universal fruits, often equated with the cantaloupe of the North, but consumed in far greater quantities. In the temperate zones its use is equally common, if unobservable to the average consumer, in the form of papain, the dried purified latex of the papaya.

People of the tropics for centuries have wrapped their meat in papaya leaves, letting it sit overnight to become tender. Modern science cubbyholed the practice as superstition. Until it discovered the papain seeping out from the leaves actually did tenderize the meat. Then, presto, a big industry. Today you can buy powdered papain in almost any store under the various brand names for meat tenderizer.

But that's only the beginning. It is also used in chewing gum along with chicle, another latex, from the sapodilla. I haven't exactly reached the stage where I'll plant gum to get a sapodilla tree. But they are very attractive trees, and I'll think of some way one of these days to get a few of the brown-sugar-flavored fruits from which to legitimately extract seeds.

If you don't chew gum and don't use meat tenderizer, chances still are you have imbibed papain in some form. Many vegetable juices have papain added to clarify them, and approximately 80 percent of all the beer brewed in the United States is stabilized and chill-proofed with it.

Then there's always toothpaste. Many of the smile-brighteners contain papain, as do some skin creams, lotions, and freckle removers. Medicinally, it is widely used for gastric distress.

The industrial uses are just as numerous. Textile manufacturers use it to de-size fabrics. Pocketbook makers, shoe producers, and other leather users tan hides with it. It is also sold as a spot remover.

When I narrated this impressive list to Susan, she eyed the full-page newspaper spread of papaya seeds in semipermanent residence on the kitchen sideboard with new interest, and dryly suggested we might trim the pile down by threading the de-ariled seeds into necklaces.

"Party favors for our next guests," she explained hopefully. "New gimmick. They could take them home and wear them around while they're germinating. You could call it the 'living necklace.'"

None of this long list, nor Susan's botanically impractical suggestion, helped my poor papaya plantation. But my next crop, perversely, weathered the critical seedling stage with flying colors. By using extra fertilizer, letting them have plenty of sun now that they were beyond the seedling state, and being extra careful not to overwater them, I was sure I could maintain a respectable papaya patch after all. They were growing much more slowly than I had expected, but I shrugged it off as the price one pays for being an apartment dweller.

I was more right than I knew. Their stunted rate of growth became more painfully obvious with the passing months. Often a papaya would stop growing entirely, its new leaves remaining small and whole rather than palmatifying, that is, dividing themselves into their proper indented shapes. Then about a month later, having lost its more mature leaves, the plant would give up the ghost. There seemed to be no conceivable cause for this. The soil was sterilized and not moist enough to produce root rot. There were goodly quantities of light and fertilizer. In desperation I finally contacted the University of Hawaii College of Tropical Agriculture. They were sure to know what was wrong.

Dr. Ivan W. Buddenhagen, chairman of their Department of Plant Pathology, solved my problem—or rather, defined it as insolvable. Papayas are very sensitive to ethylene, a common constituent of automobile exhaust and industrial waste. "I suspect," he wrote, "that your air in New York is sufficiently impure so that air pollution products may be your problem."

So in all likelihood my poor papayas were being polluted to death. And while friends of mine, living apart from the industrial heartlands, could raise their papayas to almost unmanageable sizes in proportion to their rooms, I would have to be content with my diminutive ones. Not only that, but every time I stepped out into the street in the morning and was greeted by lungfuls of chewable air, I wondered if my anemic papayas were trying to tell me something. . . .

The one thing I discovered that did seem to lift their spirits a little was keeping the humidity high. Susan was valiantly struggling to clean the window of at least a layer or two of New York soot one day, and I was making sympathetic and grateful noises, since left alone for even a month between the window cleaner's visits, the windows acquire an opaque look not conducive to the best plant growth. Suddenly I realized she was washing the windows with an absolutely indispensable gardening tool. It was a spray bottle, a nonaerosol, push-with-your-finger type, and she was just standing there placidly spraying it at the window. I kept my eye on it till she was finished and watched to see which shelf it resided on. As soon as the opportunity presented itself, I took the bottle and discreetly emptied its contents into a jar. I rinsed it out well with hot water. *Voilà*, a jungle mister.

Using warm, almost hot, water—the water temperature is reduced sharply by evaporation as it leaves the spray bottle nozzle—I bathed my jungle with a mild mist. The papayas seemed to take to it happily, and I made it a daily habit with them, but early in the morning so the sun didn't hit the plants directly until the water had evaporated. If the sun shines directly on leaves laden with water droplets, the leaves tend to turn yellow or brown.

I did my merry finger exercise quite often. Spraying with an occasional morning mist is good for almost all tropical plants. Sometimes I gave mine an evening dew, too, when I felt particularly frustrated. It makes a pretty good tension-releaser, if you can keep a sense of humor about it. Of course one can get a little too frustrated sometimes. After one particularly harrowing day I came home and headed straight for the jungle. Four bottles of mist later I felt a soft tap on my shoulder. Turning, I found Susan dressed in her rain slicker. Somewhat plaintively she remarked, "But it never rains in other apartments."

15

The Likeable Litchi from the Land of Jade

Our neighborhood boasted an excellent Chinese restaurant. The menu listed over two hundred main dishes. The desserts, on the other hand, as in most true Chinese establishments, were limited to such standard fare as fortune cookies, kumquats, and ice cream. So we were surprised on one occasion, after stuffing ourselves on Three Meats Sizzling Rice Soup and Mou Sou Pork and planning to skip dessert, to find the monotony broken by the serving of litchi (or lychee; I prefer the former, as it coincides with the botanical name, *Litchi chinensis*) nuts. Surreptitiously I slipped the seeds into one of the small plastic bags I am in the habit of carrying with me for such potential horticultural finds.

The poet Su Tung-po, living in exile in Canton, declared that the litchi would reconcile anybody to eternal banishment. To reconcile himself to his banishment, Su Tung-po devoured around three hundred litchis a day. He was careful to point out that he was a man of moderation; others unfortunate enough to be exiled to Canton drowned their woes in as many as a thousand a day.

Now I admit that, while I found the litchi nuts quite good, half a dozen or so satisfied me. Nevertheless, I dutifully planted my seeds, using a very loamy mixture, a little more

than half humus, to which I added a couple of tablespoons of sand, and the rest soil.

In its native habitat of China, the litchi is usually grown along the banks of canals, ponds, or rice paddies. The plant needs a constant supply of water and thus will not grow well on hillsides. At the same time, as is often the case with tropical plants, it also needs very good drainage. Left standing in a muddy, undrained pot for even two or three days, the plant is likely to die. The water keeps oxygen from reaching the roots of the plant and it literally suffocates to death. But suffocation wasn't the immediate problem with my plants—they just didn't develop. I had another batch of neurotic seeds that didn't know enough to germinate.

By some accounts the litchi has been cultivated as an important crop in China, particularly in the southern coastal provinces of Kwangtung and Fukien, for over four thousand years. From the looks of things it was going to take that long for me to have any plants at all. Of course, it gave us a good excuse to go out for dinner. Four months, eight Chinese dinners, an acquired taste for litchi nuts, and sixteen bare pots later, there was still no visible progress.

The impasse, as well as the difference between Su Tung-po's enthusiasm and mine, was explained to me by an exchange student from Taiwan. What we had been eating was the dried fruit, which, he pointed out, is like comparing a stale raisin with a fine chilled Muscat grape. Not only that, litchis retain their viability for a very short time. Four to five days after removal from the fresh fruit, the seed is dead. The kernels in dried litchi nuts are several months beyond resuscitation.

Now where was I going to get fresh litchis—even in New York, where you can get almost anything? The emperor Kao Tsu, who reigned with a malevolent craving for litchis about 200 B.C., used to have them relayed from southern China to Peking by runners. They were packed, sprinkled with a salt solution, in joints of bamboo. The toll in human life was said to be fantastic. I didn't approve of his methods. Even if I did, the scheme was obviously unworkable nowadays. But Kao Tsu had his fresh litchis and I didn't.

Finally someone tipped me off that in Chinatown everybody would be selling fresh litchis—in July and August. Unfortunately, it was January. But the wait was well worth it. That summer I carried home to the cool safety of the refrigerator three bags of the red, thin-shelled fruit.

True to legend, I found fresh litchis are an exotically delicious fruit. Some people have likened them to strawberries; the comparison doesn't do justice to the uniqueness of the litchi. The delicate fruit has a fragrant, flowery taste, with an ever so slightly woody texture. Verbal description fails the fresh litchi, and in any case you'll have to try one if you're going to get seeds for planting.

If you end up addicted to litchis, however, you're still going to have to wait till summer every year to lay in a supply. Chances of your trees bearing fruit are nil. For one thing, it takes eight to ten years for them to reach that stage. For another, the trees fruit best at an altitude of a thousand feet or more, which eliminates most city apartments—except maybe a penthouse on top of the Empire State Building or the World Trade Center should they decide to put one up for rent.

Once you have fresh seeds, the litchi is among the easiest tropical trees to grow and delightful to watch. The plant bears attractive small multiple leaves, which when new are translucent red, then pale pink, white, and finally, with maturity, deep green.

Seeds from a fresh litchi germinate readily. Usually all of them will sprout, something to take into account at the very beginning. I for one find it hard to just throw out a living plant, and tropical ones are too sensitive to be transplanted outdoors, except in a few of the southern states. Luckily there have always been plenty of friends wanting to take plants off our hands. But my first sowing of litchis produced twenty-six potfuls, some singles, some four or five to a pot. We narrowed the collection down to three, a manageable number. But for a while it looked as though we would have a major, if unproductive, litchi orchard.

The most important first step in litchi culture, after, of course, the exceedingly pleasant one of devouring the fruit (saving the thin shells, by the way, for future use), is to plant the seeds as soon as you can after dinner. They can be put right into the pot in which they are expected to grow. However, if you want to watch the litchis' germination and early growth, as I did with my first batch, the seeds may be placed in a small closed container the bottom of which has been lined with several layers of wet cheesecloth. There should be no free water present, but the cloth should be good and wet. Keep the container away from direct light and excessive heat. Within a week or ten days the seeds should begin to crack open and the slightly fuzzy main, or tap-, roots emerge. Those that germinate first usually turn out to be the most vigorous plants.

If after four to five weeks nothing has happened—or seven weeks if you've planted the seeds directly in soil, since the stems will not break through the surface until well after the roots have begun to grow—chances are that that batch of seeds won't germinate. Due to circumstances beyond our control, some varieties of litchi, grafted to produce better fruit, have seeds that will not sprout. These litchis are in the minority, fortunately, and buying a second batch will usually ensure a good stand of plants.

Whether you choose to germinate the seeds in separate containers or plant them directly in soil, the oval seed itself when planted should lie horizontally under about half an inch of the light, loamy, humusy soil. Use a fairly wide pot; litchi roots like to spread close to the surface. And planting several seeds to a pot, while it tends to stunt the plants somewhat, does make for a nice stand.

Before filling the litchi pot with its soil mixture, cover the drainage hole with not only the usual bent juice can tops, but also about a one-inch layer of broken shells from the litchis themselves. They will eventually rot, providing appropriate nourishment for the growing plant. Meanwhile, before reaching the decomposition stage, this layer of litchi shells will ensure good drainage and extra aeration for the plant. A layer of the shells scattered on top of the pot will add more future nourishment while it prevents too-rapid drying of the soil.

Young litchi plants are very frost-sensitive. If you plant one in August or September, the plant should be well on its way by the first freeze. But you could still lose it almost overnight if it is kept too close to a cold winter windowpane.

Another, equal danger arising from proximity to the window is too much sunlight. The plant should receive only an hour or so of direct sunlight until it is at least three months old. Even then it will grow quite demurely, if not profusely, without too much sun. This makes it an ideal plant for a room that does not afford enough light for many other species.

Since the litchi thrives in a wet environment, the pot should be watered every other day, the quantity of water depending on conditions in the apartment. A good rule of thumb is that an hour after watering the soil should be still moist enough to cling lightly to your fingers when you press the surface, but under no circumstances should it be muddy.

Watering the soil itself is not enough for a litchi, especially if your apartment is as dry as most city dwellings. Once a week, and in the dry of the winter twice a week, the leaves of the plant should be sprayed with a fine mist, using the old finger-operated window-cleaner spray bottle. A perfume atomizer is equally handy. Make sure it is rinsed out well before converting it to a jungle humidifier, however. Plants do not take well to most chemicals.

This sensitivity to chemicals extends to fertilizers. Lacking the nutrition-producing cycle of nature, all potted plants need soil supplements occasionally. Leaving a plant's fallen leaves lying in the pot to gradually decompose keeps down evaporation and enriches the soil. But an indoor plant will need more of a soil supplement than that. The commercially prepared varieties available at your local discount store are all quite good. There are only two things to watch out for in selecting one for litchis. First, litchis like an acidic soil, so don't use a nutriment additive heavy in alkalis. Secondly, lime in any form is fatal to them.

On the whole litchis are remarkably immune to the stray garden pests that may alight on your windowsill. Orchards in the Hawaiian Islands are sometimes affected by mites. But the likelihood of your plants being infected with them is about as great as your being able to concoct the spray used as an antidote. It consists of ten ounces of nicotin sulfate and a pound and three-quarters of whale-oil soap mixed well in fifty gallons of water.

With no serious illnesses to worry about, you'll discover your litchis will be around for quite some time. In China individual trees have been said to live more than eight hundred years.

16

A Rose by Any Other Name . . .
May Be a Loquat

Roses aren't usually considered fruit. When I lived in Sweden, one of my favorite dishes was *Nypon Soppa*. Served hot or cold, the heavy, sweet soup is made from the fruit of rose bushes. That and rose water were the only examples of epicurean uses of the rose family I could think of. True, I had heard of a British army unit, whose emblem was the rose, that required each new member at an initiation ceremony to consume one flower, au naturel, but that could hardly be considered more than a ritualistic repast.

Thus while digging up new seeds to sprout, I was surprised to find out that the loquat, a yellow applelike tropical fruit the size of a supercherry, belongs to the rose family. But so, I promptly discovered, does the apple, the pear, the quince, and assorted stone fruits like the peach, as well as the raspberry, blackberry, and strawberry. All these years I'd been much fonder of the rose, or at least of its nieces and its nephews and its cousins and its aunts, than I had realized.

You can take your pick of the rose family fruits to grow on the windowsill. I picked the loquat for its more exotic image. Besides, having made a new find, I was bound to take home a big bagful, and after dessert there would be a lot of loquat seeds around—whether we took a liking to the fruit or not.

The loquat on display isn't one of the most attractive of

fruits. It bruises easily and so quite often is marred by brownish areas and small hollows. In spite of what these do to its looks, they do not impair its flavor. If anything, they accentuate the tantalizing quality of the fruit. Crab apple-like in appearance, loquats taste perhaps more like cherries than any other common fruit. In fact, loquat pie, made from the seeded, underripe fruit, has been swallowed wholesale by guests of ours as cherry pie.

Although there can be as many as ten seeds per loquat, more likely there will be between one and four, since usually several ovules fail to develop. The seeds are quite large, perhaps too large for some consumers, but they are ideal from a gardening standpoint.

Lining a closed container with wet cheesecloth, I selected and washed half a dozen of the plumpest seeds for germination. Once bedded down on their damp blanket, it took them four to six weeks to sprout. Again, the seeds that germinated first grew into the healthiest and most ambitiously leafing plants.

Once loquat sprouts have developed to the point where the primary root is a third- to a half-inch long, the seeds should be transplanted to a pot. The loquat likes a sandy loam, and one frequently fertilized. A potting mixture of one-fourth sand, one-fourth soil, and one-half humus seems to suit it best. Drill a small hole into the soil with a pencil point, then place the seed so the root goes straight down, unobstructed, into the depression and the seed itself is only half-covered with soil. It should be soaked with water the first day so the soil will settle around the root.

When the stem and first couple of leaves have developed, the seed can be completely covered over with humus. This helps keep moisture in the pot and prevents the seed from contracting various infections as it decays away. Although you can fully bury the seed right after germination under a quarter-

inch or so of humus, this method tends to slow down early growth.

The loquat grows to a small evergreen tree. In its indigenous environment, the mild-wintered, moist regions of eastern central China, around the Chekiang province, its gracefully low-branched trunk reaches a scant fifteen to twenty-five feet in height under ideal conditions. It has been grown in the States successfully in California and Florida, and will do well, in fact, almost anywhere citrus trees do.

Indoors, of course, it will be considerably smaller than its outdoor sibling. But it is a beautiful plant, especially after a few years, when its smooth, cocoa-colored bark matures and its dark branches dip in deep swirling curtseys all around it.

It requires little care besides, as with all tropical and semi-tropical plants, protection from drafts and cold windowpanes in winter. The elongated, lightly saw-toothed leaves, a tiny white down giving them a pale sheen, especially on their undersides, accept with good grace as little as an hour of direct sunlight in the summer and none in the fall. It won't grow as quickly there, but a northern window will give it a niche some plants refuse to inhabit.

One word of caution: While loquats need to be watered well, they do best in a dry atmosphere. Their natural habitat is three thousand to seven thousand feet up where, though the soil is moist, the air is not.

There is always, of course, an exception to the rule. In Japan, where it is a major cash crop, the loquat is grown along the coast, to take advantage of the milder climate there. But since it's the rule one's supposed to be guided by, not the exception, I resolved to try not to spray the loquat's leaves during my dew-making activities if I could avoid it. Occasionally I did have to take off at least a few of the coats of city grime. For this I found "dry cleaning" with a soft brush, a watercolor brush, for instance, most effective. If the leaves do have to be washed, don't expose them to direct sunlight again until they have had a chance to dry.

The loquat may be a member in good standing of the rose family, but don't expect any roses on it in a hurry. It's been known to bloom, in small fragrant, white or ivory flowers, indoors only after long years.

17

A Date with a Palm or Vice Versa

A number of semisecret rituals accompanied the germination of date pits from the earliest days of their cultivation. For a year I tried as many of those that I could ferret out from the mystic authorities on the subject as were possible within our environs—all without success. One of the ancients, Ibn Awám, stressed the necessity of planting the seed horizontally, not vertically, in soil impregnated with manure and salt. Mahrarius said to soak the seed for five days, then plant it with the ventral channel, the deep indentation running along one side of the seed, down. The phase of the moon at planting time is also extremely important; I discovered there's a knowledgeable authority backing each one.

One of the early, more detailed set of instructions on date seed germination is an ancient but undated manuscript in the collection of the eminent tropical botanist P. B. Popenoe. In it firm emphasis is put on planting the seed two cubits deep (over three feet), covering it with manure, salt, and vine leaves, and giving it plenty of irrigation. The account assured me happily that "especially if the water remain on it at night will it become fat and hasten to grow and laugh with delight over its food and its face will be wreathed in smiles."

Well, my dates weren't even wreathed in leaves, much less smiles, and I certainly wasn't smiling, either. The latter, according to Saghril, was my whole problem, since "the planter must be happy and filled with joy."

The roots of my unhappiness lay in a factor none of these pundits of the desert date had foreseen. Nowadays dates are pasteurized. Now I must admit when I think of pasteurization, I think of milk next, and usually stop there. This twosome is outdated. With our modern systems of world shipping and long-term storage, pasteurization is used to prevent spoilage of a great many food items, among them the date.

Not only had my dates been fried literally to death, they had been suffocated by sulphur dioxide, to further ensure the elimination of unwanted insects, eggs, or other spoilers. By the time they got to me, the date pits were fit for burial all right, but not with intent to grow.

The problem of acquiring viable pits seemed insoluble short of a trip to Arizona or California to pick my own dates. Or better yet, make off with one of the shoots sprouting from the base of a palm. These "suckers" are the method of propagation used by commercial growers, because they "breed true." Palms from seed, on the other hand, tend to bear less and inferior fruit, or none at all.

Then, quite unexpectedly, one December day the problem was solved. I passed a health food store advertising "nonsulphured organic fruits." Among their selection were some big fat pure dates. Meanwhile Susan, doing some Christmas shopping, discovered a department-store display of "fresh" dates, which the salesclerk assured her had not been tampered with. We both came home bearing dates.

As it turned out, it was just as well we had a double supply. The salesclerk's disclaimer to the contrary, Susan's dates must have been tampered with somehow, because they never did take. With the ones from the health food store I at last met with success—even if it had taken almost the proverbial year and a day.

I settled on the only "scientific" germination method I could find for my dates. The *Proceedings of the West Virginia Academy of Science*, Volume One, Number One, August 1926, suggested that for successful germination date seeds should be soaked in water for six to eight weeks. Period. Nothing about salt, manure, or burying them under five feet of vine leaves.

After making myself almost sick gorging my pound of dates in record time, I washed the pits thoroughly and divided them into two groups. One group I submerged completely in water. The other I put in containers lined with wet cheesecloth.

Four weeks passed and nothing developed—except a minor mold on the pits not fully submerged. Reasoning that the dry desert would hardly have mold around, for once I kept it under control, washing the seeds and changing the cloth whenever new colonies started.

In a container from the previous year's attempts with pasteurized products that I had let mold away, curious to see what would happen, I counted twenty-two different varieties of mold. Or maybe they were different versions of the same one. Whatever the case, the pits were buried under a blanket of multicolored fuzz, making their pale fellows lying still in their white beds look positively naked. I found myself eyeing them with more than my usual discreetness in plant watching.

"Honor your maternal aunt, the palm," I am told Muhammad said, referring to the date, "for it was created from the clay left over after the creation of Adam (on whom be peace and the blessings of God!)." I may not have been quite prepared to greet it as a long-lost aunt, but I was ready to show due and proper respect to the date palm if it ever germinated. I'm very fond of the desert and, from travels in North Africa, have known the vital importance of the date to these lands. It is often the main course of a meal, served with camel's milk. The date is very rich in carbohydrates (about 70 percent), but contains only about 2 percent protein and fat. The combination with

protein-rich milk makes an almost ideal diet. Some Arab tribes subsist on nothing but dates and camel's milk for months.

In the desert, dates pure and simple are the usual fare. But they are also chopped and fried in butter or oil, served with sour cream, and made into jellies and preserves. They may be pounded into paste, often with locusts or other foods. Various beverages are made from dates and from the sap of the palm. The latter when fermented becomes arrack, the water-clouding drink that looks like weak skim milk and was described by the sixteenth-century explorer Pedro Teixeira as the "strongest and most dreadful drink that was ever invented, for all of which it finds some notable drinkers." All in all, the date palm is probably more important to the desert world than the coconut palm to Oceania.

Originating in western India and the Persian Gulf, the date spread throughout Arabia before recorded history. Some competent Orientalists see the date palm region of Eridu (of old Babylonia) as the origin of the biblical Garden of Eden. From there it was carried along by invaders and counterinvaders until by early recorded history it had already been naturalized in almost all of northern Africa, southern Spain, and India.

In those early days it must have been a long time between invasion and counterinvasion, considering how long it apparently took dates to sprout and grow tall enough to avoid being trampled under by clashing armies and charioteers; after six weeks nothing had happened to my pits yet. Trying not to appear anxious, I diverted my research to soil conditions, to be ready when one finally did sprout.

Date palms grow well in soil ranging from the hard clays of the Tigris-Euphrates Delta to the sandy loam of Oman and California—a broad enough range to work with, I thought. But they want good aeration and drainage and do best when rough organic materials are incorporated into the soil. The idea of adding salt to the soil, suggested by so many of the ancient

Arab growers, probably stems from the fact that the palms will grow well in soil too alkaline for most plants. The tidal action of brackish rivers near some groves will keep the soil aerated, and it's the aeration they're after, not the salt. So I made up a potting mixture of one-half soil, one-quarter humus and the other quarter vermiculite, adding an extra 10 percent of crumbled dried leaves. I couldn't resist putting a tiny pinch of salt in one of the pots.

One day, about eight weeks after first bringing home the dates, I noticed one of the pits had a tiny white string emerging from the pinhead-sized depression on the side of the pit opposite the ventral channel. At last! I thought jubilantly.

A week later it had grown no larger. Gingerly I poked at it with a toothpick. It moved. Now I've seen plants respond quickly, the Jerusalem artichoke, for instance, but this was a little too quick. I poked it again. It curled up. Close inspection showed the pit had yielded not a root, but a tiny worm.

It was obvious the evil eye was upon my incipient date plantation. Arab growers recommend sticking a sheep's skull on a pole in the middle of the plantation to avert such calamities—and disaster in general. The best I could do at the moment was a leg-of-lamb bone left over from company dinner that I'd been steadily denuding for midnight snacks. I propped it up in the pot to which I hoped to transplant the date seedling if it ever decided to germinate.

Now I'm not suggesting a lamb bone makes any difference—but. Two days after that bone left the refrigerator and entered the pot, the first of the date seeds sprouted. It was one of those bedded on wet cheesecloth, not a submerged one. Nine weeks had gone by from the time I'd first laid them out. Later I did have some sprout in less time, using the wishbone from a chicken.

The cotyledon of a seed, a thickened part of the embryo acting as a food reserve for a seedling, usually rises aboveground, developing into seed leaves. In some cases, that of peas, for instance, it stays right where the seed was planted. In the date, however, it behaves in a very unusual fashion. It emerges from the pit all right, but then it elongates, descending into the soil as if it were a root. The true primary root is at the very tip of this burrowing cotyledon. For this reason the date seed should be planted in a pot that has plenty of growing depth.

I fished mine out of the germination jar when its root-tipped cotyledon was about half an inch long. I laid it horizontal with the root in a hole bored by a chopstick, and covered it with half an inch of soil, marking the spot with a toothpick.

A month later Susan mentioned that my toothpick seemed to be thriving. Taking a look, I noticed what she meant. There were now two toothpicks, one shorter than the other. During the next week the short one continued to rise, white as ever. A singularly odd color for a palm, I thought. All this time, as I concluded from poking around experimentally with my later specimens, the root had been winding ever deeper, probably to four or six inches down.

This round-Robin-Hood's-barn behavior of the cotyledon, making like a root, can try the patience of any after-dinner gardener. But think of it from a date's point of view for a moment, and you realize the cotyledon's devious subterfuge is a kind of stubborn, brave act against overwhelming natural odds. Carrying the sensitive growing roots well below the surface of what ought to be bleak desert protects them from the hot, dry soil of the surface.

At last the toothpick began to turn green and widen out in accordion pleats, and I knew I was home. It remained only to give it tender loving care to keep it well. Its one real weakness when young is chills. The mature date palm can withstand surprisingly cold temperatures; Huntington, a botanist with extensive field experience, mentions seeing date palms in what was then called Persia when twenty inches of snow lay on the ground. But what they like best is a night-and-day temperature of a hundred degrees Fahrenheit. I couldn't offer mine that, so they settled amicably on an average of seventy-four degrees.

Give them a sunny spot and plenty of fertilizer, preferably accompanied by an occasional layer of crushed leaves broken gently into the soil, and date palms will do their magnificent best. Having less of the first to offer than they'd like, I came to terms with the fact that mine would never reach their proper regal height of a hundred feet or so, and was happy to rest under the more diminutive but still graceful shade of indoor-sized palms.

18

The Honey Berry Sour as a Lime

One thing tropical fruits seem to specialize in is having more names than an exiled Russian count waiting tables at the Waldorf. An excellent example is the quenepa. Not that I'm certain who exactly uses that particular name.

Browsing through an open Spanish market one morning, Susan and I came across a box filled with gray-green fruit about the size of small plums. Scribbled on its side was QUENEPAS. An obvious find. Neither of us had ever heard of them, much less seen one before.

Not wanting to display our ignorance, we bought a pound and scurried around the corner to eat them. We were hoping for some seeds, of course. But we got more than we bargained for this time. Peeling the leathery skin off a sample pair, we were left with a pit apiece. Nothing else to speak of, just a big pit. It was surrounded by a thin layer of what looked like corrugated Jell-O.

Obviously the next step was to try to eat it—somehow. I popped mine in my mouth and rolled it around experimentally. The flavor could be sucked off, but not much else. To boot it was *very* puckery.

"Yum," I told Susan encouragingly.

We walked around with companionably pursed lips for the rest of the afternoon. Still, the pits looked eminently plantable.

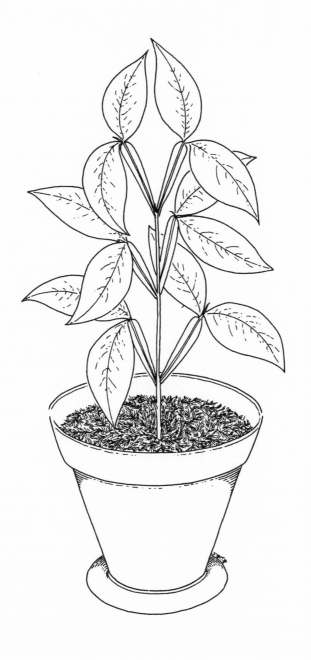

Once home I scrubbed off as much of the clinging flesh as I could with a toothbrush and warmish water. I put four seeds in a small closed container lined with the usual wet cheesecloth. Then I went to the Botanical Gardens in search of the identity of what we had just eaten and hopefully were about to grow on the windowsill.

Nobody had heard of the quenepa. None of the books mentioned it. I was about to give up when I discovered a volume called *A Dictionary of Plant-Names*, by H. L. Gerth van Wijk. The book had been published by Martinus Nijhoff at The Hague in 1916. Somewhat dated, it is still by far the best book I've found for correlating all the obscure popular names of tropical fruits with their equally obscure Latin names—the key to finding anything in botany books. For instance, a date palm is rarely listed as such, but you'll find a lot on *Phoenix dactylifera*. The quenepa, which van Wijk spelled "quenepe," turned out to be *Melicocca bijuga*.

The quenepa's proper name was derived from the Greek *meli*, meaning "honey," and *kokkos*, meaning "berry." The first half of it was all wrong. Either that or I was on a false scent.

Further research using the key Latin name—even if this one was derived from the Greek—produced the fact that in some areas it was known as the "Spanish lime." This, if not entirely accurate in my mind, certainly was coming closer to the gustatory reality. In another volume it turned up as *mamoncillo*, a "very popular fruit in Cuba and other Caribbean islands," where, I was informed, it is eaten out-of-hand, or its seeds sometimes roasted like chestnuts. The nearest verbal equivalent to my quenepa, outside of the *Dictionary*, was a Puerto Rican *genipe*. So I never did find out where the merchant we bought ours from got the name. As likely as not it's known as a quenepa in the village where he was raised, and nowhere else.

My reading warned me that the *Melicocca bijuga* in all its various linguistic versions—or quenepa to me—was a slow-growing tree. In spite of this, it took only six weeks for the pits to germinate. Compared to the trials and tribulations I had with dates, this seemed like almost overnight. The effect was achieved, directly contrary to my natural tendency, by letting sleeping seeds lie. A watched seed never sprouts, etcetera. The most circumspect approach to a germinating corner is to stroll by it with a casual over-the-shoulder glance no more than once a week. Suddenly one day there is a shining white root breaking through some seed. You can't miss it.

For after-dinner purposes the quenepa is a very handy little plant, even if as a dessert it leaves something—mostly edible fruit—to be desired. It has no special soil requirements, and while it is an underachiever compared to the really prolific plants, it makes up for it in prettiness. The multiple leaves are a bright chartreuse when they first come out on long winged stems; they later turn a deeper green.

For the patient grower there are further rewards. The quenepa will flower indoors after a number of years. The greenish white flowers, though small, are very fragrant. While the fruit may not taste like honey—the fruit of some species is sweeter than that we were introduced to—the scent of the flowers comes much closer to fulfilling the promise of the quenepa's technical name.

Quenepas have even "been known to bear fruit under glass," a properly botanical euphemism for after-dinner gardening, in the north. However, if you have leanings in this direction, I'd recommend starting at least half a dozen trees at the same time. Some of the quenepas are bisexual; most are not. And you're not going to get anywhere with, say, four males or four females, which for some perverse reason is the way they usually sort out in groups of fewer than half a dozen.

When I first started quenepa-growing, I noticed the pattern of leaves looked vaguely familiar. Looking about my jungle, I spotted another set very like it, the litchi. Sure enough, the litchi and the quenepa turned out to be related. Also in the family are the longan and the rambutan.

These two I've not yet unearthed. But the ramifications for after-dinner gardening are obvious. There are new tastes to be cultivated all the time, and as the jet age reduces distances faster and faster, it seems inevitable that the most unheard-of fruits will eventually all appear on the city dweller's table. And of course in the window garden as well.

19

"But I Want to Take a Bath":
Or, Some Problems with
Difficult Species

During my childhood the coconut became a symbol of the tropical isles and all the wonders of Oceania. In the well-thumbed books secreted in the crow's-nest of my climbing tree, a selection from Robert Louis Stevenson, Nordoff and Hall, and, my favorite, Frisbie, coconut palms usually grew along low-lying coastal areas. There was a reason for this, either I was told or I read in some source long since forgotten. The coconut, its seed too heavy for birds to carry, bobbed its way endlessly through the tropics on the ocean's currents.

So coconuts became for me romantic messengers, nature's drifting bottles carrying not SOS's, but promises of excitement and adventure. Wherever we traveled by sea, and even later, working on a deep-sea trawler, I acquired the dubious reputation of being a coconut nut by insisting, whenever an unidentifiable object floated by in our wake, that it was a stray coconut.

With such daydreams, and little chance of going to the South Seas in the near future, it was obvious that sooner or later I would have to grow a coconut palm myself. To guarantee at least one sprouting palm, I brought home seven of the biggest brown coconuts to be found at the local fruit stand. I filled the bathtub with water and added twenty heaping tablespoons of salt. The same nebulous information source that had explained the coconut's cosmopolitan distribution via the ocean waves had stressed that it wouldn't germinate unless permeated with salt water—it had to float around in the ocean at least two months before being washed ashore or it wouldn't sprout.

I dragged a chair into the bathroom, by the tub, and climbed up with my bag of coconuts. One by one, I dropped the nuts from as high as I could reach, to simulate falling from a tree. After watching them bob in the tub for a few minutes, I withdrew to the living room to reread nostalgically Hall's *The Forgotten One and Other True Tales of the South Pacific* while my coconuts drifted contentedly in circles.

By the time Susan came home I was thoroughly engrossed in the book and no longer within the confines of our New York apartment. She draped around several yards of material she'd bought for a coat, and I made appropriate, if somewhat distant, noises of approval. Studying my dreamlike stupor for a moment, she gave up, mumbling something about feeling tired and grimy from pounding the pavements and taking a shower. Five minutes later I looked up and observed her confronting me, arms akimbo, across my ottoman. I smiled innocently.

"The bathtub seems to be full of coconuts," she said.

"Uh-huh."

"They going to be there long?"

"About two months." I closed the book gingerly on my finger. "Why?"

"Oh nothing, I just thought I might want to take a bath— before next year."

I suggested soothingly that she could take the coconuts out for the duration of her bath, fill up the tub again with cool water, add twenty tablespoons of salt, making sure to mix well, and seven coconuts. I pointed out she could keep them in the sink while she used the tub.

Susan nodded understandingly, but I thought I detected a

definite gleam of mutiny in her eye. I returned to the South Pacific, the gurgling of the bathtub suggestive of an approaching typhoon.

Some weeks later the brown fibrous coconuts had acquired a decidedly slippery feel, but nothing else. I shook them. The milk was still sloshing around inside. Probably it was quite a bit cooler in our bathtub than where coconuts normally soak, I reasoned, so it could well take another couple of months. Susan didn't think so. Two months to the day of my coconut-launching, she marched into the living room after dinner with a carton full of soggy coconuts. She put it on my lap.

"Bathtubs," she announced, "are for people."

Well, maybe I had been using the wrong approach. I decided to look a bit deeper into the problems of coconut cultivation.

Most of my fondest dreams were devastated by research. Not only did the coconut not have to be permeated by salt water in order to sprout—this idea might have come from the fact that the palms will subsist in soil permeated with brackish water containing a high concentration of salt—but, according to *Tropical and Subtropical Agriculture*, by Ochse, Soule, Dijkman, and Wehlburg, there is even "some question as to whether the coconut can maintain itself in a wild state, or is merely a crop plant pure and simple." So much for the romantic cradling of the ocean's currents.

Furthermore, a coconut that has been broken free of its thick outer husk never can germinate. The husk is an integral part of the seed and its sole source of nourishment, particularly potash, for several months following germination.

In commercial plantations, large, well-matured nuts are planted lying horizontal, about two-thirds covered in loose rich soil. They have to be exposed to some light. Totally buried, the seed, like that of an avocado, will not germinate.

The first sprout makes its appearance roughly two months

after a seed is planted. The nourishment in the nut itself helps sustain the plant through its first year of growth. For most of this time the leaves remain whole, only later splitting into the familiar palm fronds.

The palm remains trunkless, contenting itself with sending out more and more leaves for several years until a crown is built up the diameter of a mature trunk. With each successive layer of green built onto the crown more roots are spread out from the thickening base until by the time the crown finally begins to rise there may be as many as four thousand separate roots. A mature tree may have as many as seven thousand, all of which help to keep the palm from blowing over in the loose sandy loam it prefers.

Very nice, but where in the city was I going to find a "large, well-matured" coconut complete with husk?

The problem resolved itself in an unexpected way. My mother had been sick that summer and by vacation time was still not able to travel far. So my father took her to Florida to laze on the beach. I've never been all that interested in the Miami area; I perused their postcards—showing a series of high-rise hotels and kidney-shaped swimming pools three feet from the ocean's edge—only far enough to determine that all was well.

My father had a habit of summing up a situation with put-on folk sayings. So his cryptic note, "Confucius say of Florida, 'Nuts to you,'" registered in my mind only as his mild protest against having had to cancel their original plans to explore the Yucatán Peninsula. I was thus totally unprepared for the shock of finding he had spent the entire return flight with a large, well-matured, and slightly sprouting coconut lolling nonchalantly on his lap.

As I discovered in the weeks following my parents' fruitful trip, the coconut is an ideal plant for the apartment dweller. It's been far too long ignored.

The only drawback is its need for a very sunny warm spot. For commercial growth, I understand, coconuts require a mean temperature of at least eighty degrees Fahrenheit. But I found that as long as there's plenty of sun they will grow, if not at their lushest, with an average temperature of seventy-two to seventy-five degrees. Most apartments have a spot somewhere that can be kept this warm. In winter, however, the coconut will have to be watched closely. By a window it will be much colder, even as far as a foot from the pane, than you would expect.

If you get hold of a large coconut in its husk—and I've noticed some places sell them now as novelties—there is about a one-in-four chance you can get it to germinate. Next to selecting the biggest and ripest one you can find, the most important step is to make sure that wherever it sits, it's propped up so the fat end is about two inches higher than the pointed end. I don't know where they developed their finicky attitude towards posture, but coconuts are apt not to germinate unless resting at an angle of about ten degrees, depression end up. Maybe it stems from the fact that the depression is the first part of the husk to decay, letting in more water.

The properly propped coconut, set in a pan, should be sprayed lightly with water every day, particularly around the hollow. The two main watering places for a coconut are the crack through which the sprout pushes its way and, before that happens, this depression at the fat end by which the nut once hung, acornlike, from the palm. The depression will respond to watering almost like a sponge. Give it all it wants every other day.

To give the incipient roots the feeling they have somewhere to go, it's a good idea to fill the pan in which the coconut rests with an inch or so of moist sand. This homemade beach also makes it easier to keep the nut at the proper angle.

By the time a second leaf has sprouted, the coconut is defi-

nitely ready for some real soil. Roots may already be breaking through the husk before this, in which case plant it right away, even if it has as little as one undeveloped leaf showing. Delayed planting tends to aid and abet stunting, a tendency that indoors already manifests itself too readily because of less than ideal conditions.

The nut should be only partially buried, about two-thirds, slanted at the same angle as before. Plastic five-gallon cans and redwood tubs are about the only pots big enough for coconuts. But whatever container you use, make sure it has sufficient drainage. The reason the coconut palm thrives so happily along low-lying coasts, however salty, is that the tides constantly raise and lower the water table of the porous soil, aerating it. Like many tropical plants, the coconut does not develop those almost microscopic hair roots you see on plants native to the temperate zones, and even with its massive system of larger roots it has trouble absorbing enough oxygen without this changing groundwater level.

To ensure a soil that is both loose, permitting good aeration, and rich enough to sustain the palm, use a mixture of one-fourth vermiculite or rough sand, one-fourth potting soil, and one-half humus. It is important to plough up the soil with a fork to a depth of three to four inches each week or so, to prevent caking.

Never spray a coconut's leaves when watering. Although in its natural habitat the palm's leaves are often soaked in ocean spray, this is accompanied by winds which evaporate the water away quickly. The robust leaves are not affected by the salt, so no damage is done. But a prolonged period of dampness, as would follow indoor spraying, tends to foster fungi, themselves invisible but causing the leaves to develop yellow splotches, eventually turning brown, giving them a burned look.

Twice a month the palm should be watered so heavily that

a pool collects in the tray beneath the pot. But be sure to empty the tray afterwards. Better yet, since the waterlogged pot will be heavy, rest it on a layer of stones, or a double layer of marbles, which will act like a set of worn-out ball bearings when you turn the pot. Then water dripping out will not stay in contact with the bottom of the pot, which would promptly reabsorb it again.

Watering plants occasionally by osmosis from the bottom up is a good idea in general, if done with temperance. But if the soil becomes too saturated by heavy watering, from either above or below, and the pot is left sitting in a puddle in its drainage dish, the standing water will rot the roots and sour the soil, killing the plant. This is especially true for coconuts and other tropical plants.

Watering my coconut so heavily twice a month, I found it necessary to fertilize it more often than other plants. Nutritive substances in the soil are water-soluble, which is how they are absorbed by the plant. This also means that when water drains right through a pot it takes along some of the nourishment with it. This leaching out of the soil can only be offset by good fertilization.

By the time a palm is a year old, it will have a number of large leaves, some finally beginning to split into the frondlike structure of the mature leaf. It is ready for a higher ground level, achieved by adding enough soil to cover the exposed third of the nut, which by now should be decaying away. The new layer of soil does the most good if it is made specially rich. A trip to the local mounted police for some horse manure would really be ideal at this point. It's the perfect accessory, ploughed into the soil before the additional layer is applied. Susan, however, put her foot down on manure in our small living room in winter, and talked me into using an extra-richly fertilized mixture of potting soil and humus instead. It worked just as well, actually.

There's not a chance in the world of getting your coconut palm to flower indoors, much less bear fruit. You'll never become a self-made "copra baron" that way. This most valuable derivative of the coconut, copra, the dried meat of the ripe nut, was the main cargo hauled by the much-romanticized inter-island schooners that used to ply the Pacific under full sail. Although it takes an awful lot of coconuts (well over five thousand) to make a ton of copra, it is so rich in vegetable oil that the lucrative copra trade flourished in spite of the size limitations on sailing ships and all the hardships and dangers involved.

Schooners have long since lost their place in the economic limelight; copra has not. It is used in the compounding of medicines, the manufacture of soap, margarine, and a number of other commodities requiring high-grade oil. The pressed cake remaining after the oil has been extracted from copra is high in protein, sugar, and vitamins, and makes excellent cattle fodder. The coconut husks are saved as well, either for mulch or, more recently, for making into a light-colored fiber.

On an individual human basis, however, perhaps the most significant value of the coconut is still as a staple eaten out-of-hand. In the late 1950s it was estimated that some four hundred million inhabitants of the tropics depended on the coconut as their sole or major source of fat. The same study estimated the annual world production of coconuts at nearly two billion. Both figures startled me right out of my daydreams of coconut schooners drifting lazily in clear blue lagoons, waiting to take on a cargo of a couple thousand nuts.

There are still countless weary vagabonds in the tropics to whom a coconut grove comes into view as the oasis does to a desert traveler. Thankfully they will pause in their travels to gather a coconut, lob off the top with a swift slice of the machete, and drink the cool, thirst-quenching and nourishing coconut milk. Along unnumbered equatorial beaches Gatorade has nothing on the coconut.

So maybe it was economic justice that the coconut should bear in tropic corners and not in mine. In any case, I decided my palm suited my window just fine the way it was, and had the added advantage of not dropping one of two billion coconuts unexpectedly on one of New York's eight million heads— with those kinds of numbers involved, chances would be pretty high.

20

Yes, We Have No Bananas: Or, Cheating a Little

I remember the first time I drove through Miami, Ohio. I was visiting a friend newly moved there, and up to then I had never heard of a Miami in Ohio, assuming there was only one, it naturally belonging to Florida. What confused matters even more was that right smack in the middle of the lawn across the way from my friend's house was a banana tree. Not in a hothouse or anything, just in the middle of the lawn, like a diminutive flagpole waving a lot of green flags. During the winters I had spent in Ohio, the temperature used to go down to ten below zero; the banana tree was too big to take indoors, and it wasn't made of plastic.

All of which added up to "a puzzlement"—until I found out it was in a buried pot and the owner cut the plant down to within a few inches of the soil every fall and put it in the basement next to the oil burner for the cold winter. By that time the banana would have a batch of suckers sprouting around the main stalk. These he would cover over with mulch during their basement seclusion. Come spring, he would let the new shoots stretch in a warm sunny window before taking the pot outdoors again. Suddenly, overnight, his lawn would be sporting a new waving banana plant.

I never did find out where he got the original plant—something I lived to regret. Because when the after-dinner garden

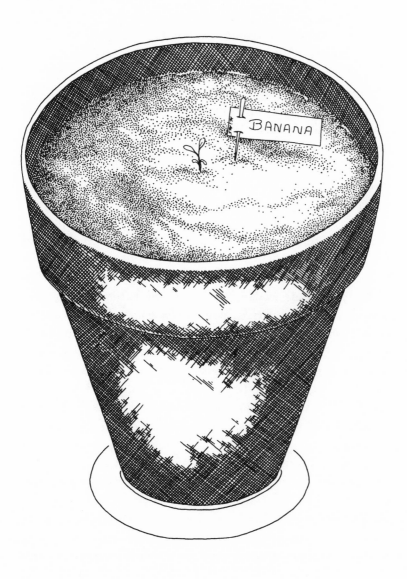

bug bit me, one of the things I wanted most to grow was a banana plant. And what a struggle that was!

My first approach to the species was to a local bunch of the plumpest, ripest Chiquita bananas to be had. Viewing them with a critical eye not formerly interested in the botanical makeup of the banana, I was struck by the similarity of the inside of a banana to the inside of a Chinese gooseberry. That is, when one looked closely, there were several ribs of the tiny seeds running lengthwise through the fruit. Of course they were terribly small, but then, so were those of the Chinese gooseberry, and they had sprouted eventually. After picking the seeds carefully out of several halved bananas, I disguised the pockmarked remains, with great gobs of trimmings, as banana splits.

The minuscule seeds I carefully dried on tissue paper for a day and then transferred, half to wet cheesecloth-lined containers and half to a pot of nice rich soil, covering those with an eighth-inch of humus.

I was planting plenty, because I didn't really hold out much hope for the Chiquitas; they had been specially bred for a beautiful banana, with seeds so as you wouldn't notice them when you ate it, and with superior handling and keeping qualities for carefree shipping, while the plant itself was developed to be highly disease-resistant and relatively low-growing so as not to be damaged readily by winds. Not surprisingly, somewhere along the way the Gros Michel, as this banana variety is known, lost much of its flavor. The gold-backed darling of the United Fruit Company and other American banana importers is about the equivalent of paper pulp in taste compared with cultivated species of the Far East and elsewhere. In Indonesia, for instance, it is considered so inferior it is fed only to babies, who presumably don't know enough to argue.

Be that as it may, I soon found out my problem wasn't going

to be getting a tastier banana to grow from Chiquita seeds, but rather getting anything to grow from them at all. The brown banana specks I had so carefully tended turned out to be aborted seeds from ovules never fertilized.

The beginnings of the banana are buried somewhere in southern Asia and, because thousands of variants developed over the centuries, the exact location and type of the parent plant will probably never be unearthed. Nevertheless, the fact remains that many of the edible bananas—whose names cover a vast range, Creole Banana, Saint Pierre Banana, Black Banana, Plumed Banana, Horn Banana, Eyeless Banana, Red Fig Banana, and *Go-sai-heong* (meaning "perfume that descends from the mountains" in Chinese), to make just a start on the list—do have proper, plantable seeds, in assorted sizes. Unfortunately, the fact also emerges that even more of these countless edible bananas are "seedless."

Some botanists believe that primitive bananas with fertile seeds were cultivated in ancient times not only for the fruit, but for the tender heart of the plant itself, still used as food in Ethiopia today. That banana plants were among the earliest of cultivated crops is fairly well agreed upon. Exactly how long ago that was is still a question. Beccari, for instance, believes they were an important cultivated crop as early as the Pliocene epoch (spanning the period from one to ten million years ago). But since paleontologists aren't exactly sure that humans as we think of them existed then, and botanists aren't sure that the banana as we know it existed, either, it seems fruitless to carry the speculation any further.

At any rate, P. Popenoe, in *J. Heredity* (1914), Volume 5, page 273, attributed the development of the modern "seedless" banana to hybridization of wild "diploid" varieties, or, plants having two sets of similar chromosomes. As often happens with hybrids, these produced sterile plants. But things didn't end there, for the banana's fortunate latent talent for producing offspring by means of suckers came to the fore, and from the sterile plants new little sterile plants sprang, and so on.

The new seedless banana in all probability wouldn't have gotten very far. Although the birds feasting on the seeded variety would end up scattering banana seeds for miles around, they would have nothing to do with transporting suckers. They were just as happy eating seedless bananas, of course, but that didn't do the suckers a whit of good in thumbing a ride anywhere.

People were just as happy eating seedless bananas, too, if not happier. Then again, they would just as soon have a banana plant growing next to their hut as walk three miles for breakfast. Having a choice between moving their residence to the banana and moving the banana to their house, people naturally chose the latter. At least that's the assumption. They dug out some small suckers from a banana patch and took them home to replant. Borne along by such pragmatic reasoning, the banana spread slowly and surely throughout the aeons across all of southeast Asia, finally reaching the Pacific during the first Polynesian migration about the time of Christ.

All of which would imply that the logical approach to banana planting would be to study some rudimentary forms of *musa*, the species to which bananas belong, checking particularly how they flower and fruit. That way I should at least come up with enough facts to calculate the odds on finding a banana with fertile seeds. The only handy reference to a study on the floral morphology of the banana was to an article by P. R. White in Z. *Zellforsch. mikroskop. Anat.* (1928), Volume 7, page 673—a classic, I'm told, though you can't prove it by me. I couldn't get through the title, much less the contents. So much for the logical approach.

Besides, by now I had found some dwarf "wild" bananas at a fruit stand. On examination, I must admit, their seeds didn't seem much more promising. They were the same size as the others actually, even if proportionately, judged by the size of their banana, they were bigger. Going through the same extraction process, I dutifully planted them. Much to my surprise, five weeks later a small green shoot rose in the center of the pot. It was only about half an inch tall, but to my frustrated and overwrought imagination the leaves were definitely, at least in prototype, "bananaish."

Susan would have none of my "dwarf banana plants start out small" theory and remained a firm disbeliever. Without even bothering to give my "minibanana" another look, she bet me a home-baked banana cream pie, one of my favorites, it was no cousin of a *musa*. I lost. But Susan's winnings weren't exactly what she'd expected. While I bake a pretty mean apple pie, for some reason banana cream does not fall into my range of expertise. It tends to develop a texture akin to axle grease.

That was the night when, at three o'clock in the morning after Susan had bravely devoured a large portion of my pie, I was awakened by a sharp elbow in my rib cage.

"Plantains!"

Maybe Susan was wide awake, due, I maintained, to the gastric consequences of her wager, though she stoutly denies it, but I wasn't, and I proceeded to roll over.

Another elbow in my ribs, followed by the inevitable "Plantains!"

By now I was pestered enough to manage a "Huh?"

"Plantains, you know, those big green cooking bananas. I think I remember them having bigger seeds."

There'd been times when I was happy there were twenty-four-hour grocery stores in our neighborhood. Then again, there'd been times when I wasn't particularly. This was one of them. It was the middle of January and five degrees out. The bed was warm and comfortable. There were no more rib ticklers. But sleep had gone the way of the wild banana.

We stopped on our way back with our bag of plantains, for ham and eggs. One might as well start the farm chores in the wee small hours after a hearty breakfast. When we got home I prepared and planted the seeds, which were indeed a little bigger. But these too never did sprout. The subject of plantains was not brought up again in our house, and for a while we went back to eating exclusively regular "uncooking" bananas.

The homely banana, forever associated in some American minds with slicing over cereal, has apparently been linked with the ready-mix breakfast idea since long before the days of freeze-drying. Going back to the twelfth century, in fact, I found Fan-Ch'êng mentioning, in his *Kuei-hai yü-hêng chih* (in translation, of course), that bananas can be preserved by being soaked in sugared plum juice, dried, and then pressed flat. Crystals of sugar remain on the outside, "frost," as Fan-Ch'êng puts it, giving a pleasant sweet-and-sour taste.

Although the plant itself originates in the Indo-Malay region, the term "banana" is of African origin. Here, too, the fruit was thought worth preserving even by pre-refrigerator methods. H. M. Stanley, in his book *In Darkest Africa*, mentioned a banana flour ground from the dried fruit. "If only the virtues of the flour were publicly known," he wrote, "it is not doubted that it would largely be consumed in Europe. For infants, persons of delicate digestion, dyspeptics and those suffering from temporary derangement of the stomach, the flour properly prepared would be in universal demand. During my two attacks of gastritis, a light gruel of this, mixed with milk, was the only matter that could be digested." Indeed it seems to me banana flour would add a different touch to the same old recipes, and I'm surprised no chef has tried to trademark it.

Attempts of a vaguely successful nature have been made to manufacture banana coffee, banana wine, and banana vinegar. Not to mention banana jam, for which I found the following commercial recipe: Take two hundred pounds of sugar, ten gallons of water and twelve ounces of cream of tartar, and boil them to two hundred and thirty degrees Fahrenheit; add two and a half gallons of lemon juice and two hundred pounds of ripe banana pulp; boil to two hundred twenty-four degrees Fahrenheit. Although a bit on the massive side, Susan thinks it would be worth trying—with peanut butter on rye.

One of the more esoteric uses of the banana was conceived during the great raisin shortage of World War II. I myself am unfamiliar with that particular deprivation, but I have been assured that it did in fact exist. Apparently it spawned "Banibs." Banibs, in case you'd never heard of them, either, were ersatz raisins made from ground dehydrated whole bananas, mixed with washed copra meal and 10 percent sugar and dry-rolled into raisin-sized pellets. However, the project never really got off the ground.

The populace of India, with no particular shortage of raisins in their past, have an uninterrupted culinary tradition in the very tasty, if difficult to pronounce, *Panchamruthan*, a confection using banana pulp and raisins, with ghee, molasses, honey, and sugar added to make sure it's sweet enough. In some regions variants of this are served in fig-sized pieces appropriately enough called "banana figs." For that matter, dried banana chunks in general are often dubbed figs.

Sixteenth-century writers referred to bananas as "Adam's figs" or "apples of paradise"; the legend was that the banana was the Tree of Knowledge in the Garden of Eden. This supports a point of mine. After reading up on tropical fruits, I've come to the conclusion that just about the only thing never suggested at one time or another as being on the Tree of Knowledge is the truffle, and that's probably only because no one thought of checking down around the roots.

But meanwhile, we were still eating bananas, all kinds, makes, and models of bananas, and still no fruitful-looking seeds in any of them. In the end, I finally admitted defeat and decided a little cheating in this case couldn't hurt—well, after all, it can only be a matter of time till they're jetting in shipments of big seedy healthy bananas direct from somewhere. I sent away for some banana seeds. These I found in the Geo W. Park horticultural catalogue, which listed two species, *M. Ensate* and *M. Arnoldiana*, and assured me that the seeds were in constant supply, preserved in hermetically sealed envelopes.

The germination time for bananas is highly erratic, anywhere from one week to four months. It's a help to them, though not a necessity, to have bottom heat. If you want to be fancy about it, special waterproof cables for this purpose can be purchased at gardening supply stores. But for the after-dinner garden I found base heat for germination pots could be provided quite effectively by a radiator top. It wasn't as constant a source of heat as the cables, but my pots didn't seem to mind that. The one addition needed when using the radiator top for base heat is a thermometer, to take the surface temperature of what the pot is sitting on. If the thermometer registers above ninety-five degrees Fahrenheit, put a layer of cardboard or thin cork under the pot and take another reading on that. Eighty to eighty-five degrees is the ideal you're aiming for, with the temperature at the top of the pot, where the seeds are, at around seventy-five degrees. Adjust the thickness of the insulating layer until this temperature range is reached with the radiator going full blast. Also, when using bottom heat you will find the evaporation rate from the pot is higher than normal, so remember to check when extra water is needed.

Banana seeds, I found, are a tough and lazy lot. One has to nick them pretty roughly and then keep them submerged underwater for twenty-four hours before they'll get down to the business of germinating. The soaking part is easy enough. But the nicking part is about like trying to scratch a diamond with your fingernail. I grudgingly admit, though I have steadfastly refused to let one in the house, that here's where an electric

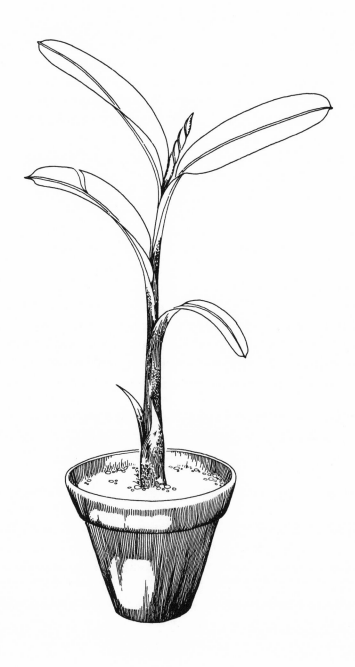

carving knife might really come in handy. After splitting two seeds completely apart and managing one very artistic nick— in my thumb—I finally achieved at least a deep scratch on a few of the seeds.

Following their twenty-four-hour soak, I laid my now docile seeds, the prominent seed scar facing up, in a bed of two-thirds humus and one-third soil. I covered them with about a quarter-inch of soil and gave them a thorough dousing. Only in surroundings kept warm and wet will banana seeds submit to growing up.

As soon as my seeds were bedded down, our visions of walking down Fifth Avenue parading a large banana leaf as the latest in umbrellas began. But while things happen fast, most of them don't happen quite that fast. Particularly not the germination of banana seeds; mine took almost six weeks. Once the first recalcitrant sprout rose, I thought it would make up for lost time. In some experiments recorded in Hawaii, the banana leaves grew three and a half to four and a half inches a day and increased in surface area from fifty-nine to sixty-seven square inches per day. Mine didn't. Being indoors and not under perfect conditions, they weren't about to break any world records. But I kept the young plants in a warm sunny spot and their steady progress soon assured me that before the Fifth Avenue rainy season I would have big enough banana leaves to keep Susan's hair dry, anyway.

Since where there's a banana plant there's always the bare chance of a sudden crop of little unexpected bananas, there is one word of warning that should be given any after-dinner plantation manager with a banana in the bunch. Sadly but truly, a lot of plants have never learned to live together peaceably. An aggressively ripening banana, intent on its own ends, heedlessly gives off ethylene. You could have real jungle warfare brought on your windowsill if the ethylene invades the air space above a papaya. The papaya, you will recall, can never abide by that. In the interests of the botanical community, therefore, it might be wise to take proper precautions against an air pollution problem before moving too many plants into any given area.

2 1

The Marmalade Patch

Every year in late fall, Susan would start the plum puddings. At the same time she would put up a good batch of assorted marmalades for the winter. With all those citrus fruit seeds beckoning from the kitchen butcher block, I could hardly resist raising a bit of company for the first little lemon tree—standing bravely alone of its kind at the edge of my now lush jungle—that had started it all.

Selecting a variety of the seeds left from Susan's preserving endeavors, I started what she was later to nickname the Marmalade Patch. The citrus fruits are a big family, and I was able to pick out and plant lemon, lime, grapefruit, and orange seeds. I thought I had a fairly representative collection till I saw the jar of citron Susan had sitting on the sideboard. The fine print on the backside label informed me that citron, which I had always supposed was just a variety of candied lemon peel, was in fact a distinct fruit. Actually the citron is cultivated almost exclusively for its peel, a rather unusual procedure; I can't think of any other fruit raised for its superior exterior instead of its interior.

The citron was one of the earliest citrus fruits to become part of European gustatory culture. It was introduced to the Mediterranean as early as 300 B.C. by the Arabs. In contrast, the now much more popular lemon is not presumed to have reached the same region until about 1100 A.D. Why this difference in traveling time arose is hard to imagine, since both fruits originated in Southeast Asia and both went to Europe by the Mediterranean route of the Arabs.

The lemon, citron, and orange originated in more or less the same Asian area. But not all the citrus fruits came from there. The grapefruit started out in the West Indies; the mandarin, in the Philippines. Whatever their origin, citrus fruits of every kind are now cultivated almost around the globe, in a wide belt spanning from thirty-five degrees north latitude to thirty-five degrees south latitude. And in making the rounds they have managed to grow in almost every conceivable kind of soil.

They prefer a loose sandy loam, however, and I decided on a soil mixture of half potting soil, half humus, and a good handful of sand, for my citrus pots. After rinsing the seeds off with tepid water, I laid them in their beds and covered them with an extra half-inch layer of humus, working it down snugly around the seeds by watering.

Young budding citrus plants cannot tolerate a drought. In addition to the regular twice-weekly watering of the pot, the topsoil should be sprayed with a bit of water every day. If the leaves develop a "wilt," caused by underwatering, they can't be counted on to recover miraculously like the Jerusalem artichokes. A drought-wilted young citrus will probably expire from shock.

Still, on the whole, citrus plants are among the easiest of after-dinner plants to grow. The majority of commercial citrus plantings are left fully exposed to the sun. A "shade crop," a quick-growing cover growth to protect species easily sunburned, is not usually thought necessary, even above the young trees. Once set out in the fields, the plants are left unshaded, even though in their native habitat they would usually be protected by a canopy of high forest trees. This easy adaptability of the citrus orchard to varying light conditions is handy indeed for apartment dwellers; it permits them to place the plants almost anywhere. In fact, I've grown some where they received no natural light at all.

There are on the market several brands of fluorescent tubes designed specifically for plant light. Although their operating life can be unpredictable—I had one that expired on me after two hours, which was frustrating, since there was no guarantee and the bulb was on the expensive side—they are excellent for growing plants just about anywhere, including the closet if you run out of space. Even without these special bulbs, successful plant lighting can be achieved by a combination of regular fluorescents, one bluish and one reddish. The one thing to be taken into account in placing fluorescent lights for your plants is that the light is considerably weaker at the ends of the tubes than at the center. Since my citrus fruits were more adaptable than some of my other plants, I put them at each end and gave the center of the stage to my more light-hungry plants, like the papayas.

Fluorescent lighting is by no means the only artificial light that can be used. Citrus grows well under an ordinary seventy-five-watt or hundred-watt incandescent bulb kept one to two feet away from the apex of the plant. In fact, I found that germination and early growth of most tropical plants is aided by keeping a seventy-five-watt lamp burning for a total of from fourteen to sixteen hours a day about a foot above the seedlings. Although a table lamp does not provide the full range of light needed for most plants to do their best, they will grow under it, and seedlings seem to appreciate the extra warmth given by the incandescent bulb, especially in winter. But make sure the plant is not so close to the bulb that its leaves dry out, and don't forget to compensate for the quicker evaporation of water from the topsoil under the lamp's heat.

Most citrus trees begin to take an interest in blooming along about their fifth year. The fruit won't ripen till ten to sixteen

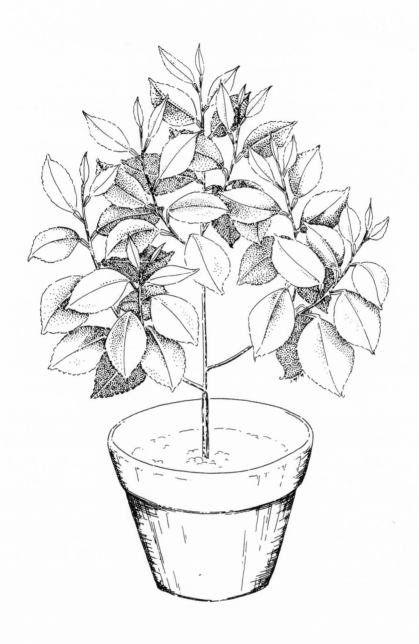

months after the flowering. Although privately I thought my chances of getting to pick any fruit from my indoor trees were pretty slim, at least I would have plenty of time to check into commercial harvesting methods before the patch decided to surprise me by coming into fruition. Oranges seemed to be the most prevalent orchard-grown citrus species, so I chose them to investigate.

Quite often, I knew, oranges are picked when green. But this doesn't mean they are unripe. Oranges can't be induced to "after-ripen," or go on ripening after they are picked, the way some fruits, for instance the banana, can. Contrary to their name, oranges are frequently green or yellowish green when fully ripe. To give them a better marketing image, the oranges are placed in a "degreening" room, where once more my dubious ally ethylene pops into the picture. Ethylene is used to accelerate the natural process known as degreening, the decomposition of chlorophyll, leaving the "orange" pigments, carotenes and xanthophylls, in the rind as the dominant colors. So far so good. Chlorophyll I knew all about from the days of the old ad campaign demonstrating its use to eliminate odors in everything from toothpaste to shoe polish. Carotenes, I remembered from high school botany, were in carrots—a much more appropriate place for them than oranges, I'd think—and were good for the eyes. Xanthophylls I'd never heard of, but I was willing to take the degreeners' word for their powers, assuming the subject had probably been researched pretty carefully by hordes of aspiring corporate fruit-company botanists.

However, things get even more complicated after the degreening room. First the oranges are scrubbed, then they're washed with soap and antiseptic, then they proceed through a moisture eliminator. Then, if they're still not orange enough, they're dyed, passed through another antiseptic solution, and waxed.

That was the point at which I chucked my investigation. With a sense of relief I turned to the remembered pleasant simplicity of orange groves in Morocco. Once after spending a night on the desert I found myself at dawn on the edge of an orange grove on an ideally located oasis. The owner invited me to pick a breakfast for myself, and I spent the morning acquiring a bellyache by twisting the still night-cooled fruit off the trees and devouring them hungrily. Without a doubt those were the most delicious oranges I've ever eaten. Not to mention the most easily harvested. Surely I could manage to pluck and enjoy the unprogressive oranges from my own trees in the same simple old-fashioned way. The price of progress seemed by comparison too complicated and too high to pay.

Another casualty of mass production is the orange wrapper. Only occasionally, in a particularly fancy gift box of fruits, do I ever catch glimpse of one. And even then, while each orange may be individually wrapped in crisp crinkly tissue paper with a seal or symbol on it, the beautiful elaborations are gone. I suppose kids can still collect stamps, as for that matter most of them did in the neighborhood where I grew up. But you'll never convince me that for a little boy a stamp book can ever hold the same bright joy that was contained in my collection of fruit wrappers. I had hundreds of them, from all over the world, and they were covered with some of the most ornate and colorful designs I've ever seen.

It's a forever-lost hobby. Nowadays most oranges aren't even eaten as oranges, much less wrapped at all. Almost 70 percent of them are made into frozen orange juice. The leftovers go into producing cattle feed, molasses, and various oils. So much for a new generation of orange wrappers.

But back to the generation of a home orchard. My trees had been growing for months before I noticed that all my citrus had thorns. Susan had mentioned them one day before, but I had dismissed them as undeveloped leaves or branching attempts. After all, who ever heard of thorny oranges? Nevertheless, thorns they have.

They also have "water sprouts." Or at least they're supposed to have water sprouts. I've never found a clue as to where the term came from. In fact, I haven't been able to figure out quite what they are in the first place. All I know for sure is that when they develop you're supposed to prune them off, as they drain growing energy from the main plant. The only, and somewhat unhelpful, definition I could find of a water sprout was in the volume that warned me against them, and read as follows: "An extremely vigorous sucker or shoot originating from the trunk or main limb of a tree, especially a fruit tree." The problem with this definition, to me, was that it made the sprout sound more like a branch than anything else, which would imply pruning off all the branches, and that didn't make sense. Whatever the case, I didn't seem to have any water sprouts on my plants. Maybe they knew they would be pruned and didn't bother to develop.

In the end I managed to fit into my plantation a representative from almost all the citrus fruits available in our neighborhood, including kumquats, incidentally one of the hardiest. Then I settled down to wait impatiently for the fruit companies to begin importing a few more distant relatives, like the White-Sapote and the Wampee. Especially the Wampee. I'd heard the fruit was nothing special, but I liked the name. Somehow it would be neat to have a Wampee tree.

22

The Unkindest Cut of All: To Prune or Not to Prune?

Every time one of my jungle additions reached the beanstalky stage, I was confronted with the same torturous decision: to prune or not to prune? Well, not quite every time. Some plants are designed to just grow straight up, for instance, palm trees, either coconut or date, or a papaya, banana, or pineapple. Pruning these, except to remove wilted leaves, would be tantamount to plant mutilation.

A somewhat general rule of thumb to follow is that plants whose leaves all spread out from one crown, or a succulent or very watery-stemmed tropical plant, will usually not be helped by pruning. Show me such a plant and I could wave the question aside with an air of confident finality. Real trees, and vines, are something else again. Here I lost my air of "papa knows best." I had a moot question on my hands.

Certainly when fruit trees are under cultivation, pruning serves a definite function. It keeps the trees more compact and the fruit within easier picking reach. In addition, shortening the main branches makes them sturdier, so they can carry a heavier crop of fruit without breaking under their weight, such breaking, I suppose, being a form of natural pruning.

But the after-dinner gardener isn't usually trying to cultivate a whole orchard on the windowsill. Here pruning becomes a matter of choice, not necessity—except, of course, in the case where a plant outgrows, or overgrows, the room, a not infrequent occurrence. According to some, pruning produces a more attractive, apartment-shaped plant. And it can't be disputed that in many cases, as with citrus trees, or the avocado, it does tend to produce a stronger, more filled-out tree.

Preferring the natural look myself, I would argue that it's more interesting to see what the plants do on their own. Will the avocado begin branching at three feet? Not too likely. At six feet? About average. At nine feet? Problems ahead. Or not even after it hits the ceiling? Definitely time to cut back! I had one lemon tree that grew straight up for three feet, then, swaying in the breeze one day, the tender shoot got seasick, I think; whatever the case, it fell off. A case of natural pruning.

Everything seems to be due to hormones these days. Plants are no exception. When a plant is cut back, or pruned, what happens next is due to a hormone called auxin, more properly known as indole-3 acetic acid, abbreviated IAA. Since I find the biochemists' specialized language, and the diagrams that go with it, highly confusing, I'll keep calling it auxin.

The presence of auxin was suspected for many years before it was actually found. Darwin, discussing the Earth's gravitational pull and its relation to plant root development, wrote "that it is the tip alone which is acted on, and that this part transmits some influence to the adjoining parts, causing them to curve downward." Nobody knew quite what this "influence" might be, but it was surmised to exist as a physical substance.

In the early 1930s Kögl and Haagen-Smit (and this was before the era of esoterically named rock groups) isolated a substance they called auxin-A, and later one they called auxin-B. But nobody else managed to find them. Unperturbed, the group took on a third person, Exleben, and went on to discover what we know as auxin today. To differentiate it from the auxins they'd found before, just in case somebody should sud-

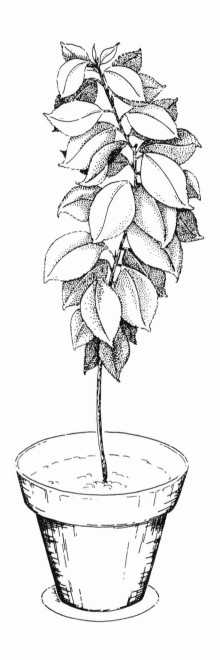

denly rediscover those, Kögl, Haagen-Smit, and Exleben called the new one heteroauxin, or "the other auxin." It was found distributed throughout a living plant, but concentrated most in the growing tips, which would include both the above-ground shoots and the roots. It wanders around in a plant all the time. More scientifically, it is translocated.

"How?" is the big question botanists still can't answer without arguing about it. Some describe it in terms of electrical charges, others in metabolic changes—all very interesting, but likely to be challenged by the next person on the quiz show. The only fact they seem to agree on is that auxin is the growth hormone for plants.

Nevertheless, even this bare fact is a help in understanding how pruning works. And the theory of "apical dominance," which has the largest number of followers at the moment, provides at least a logical framework on which to build an explanation.

1. Just the right amount of auxin, no more, no less, is needed for a plant to grow. This is the optimum amount. Either more or less auxin than the optimum amount inhibits growth. There is a minimum/optimum/maximum concentration of auxin possible in every part of the plant. In other words, either there is just enough auxin in the right place for proper growth or there is too little (the minimum) or too much (the maximum), in both of which latter cases growth will be slowed down.

2. The apical bud, the bud highest up on a plant, normally hogs the most auxin. This bud, according to the current theory, controls the growth of the whole plant, hence the name apical dominance.

3. The lateral buds, poking out sideways along the upright stem or trunk of the plant, are more sensitive to auxin than the rest of the plant. A concentration of auxin just right for the

main plant is too strong for the lateral buds and keeps them from growing. The plant grows taller, and the buds remain dormant.

4. The plant keeps growing as long as the apical bud, by whichever of the means under debate, keeps sending auxin down the length of the plant from its abundant supply. If the apical bud is cut off, taking with it the major hoard of auxin, the main plant is left with a minimum supply, and it stops growing. But the lower concentration of auxin is just right for the lateral buds and they begin to grow. Liberated branches sprout enthusiastically along the sides of the plant.

5. Basically, however, the plant prefers a state of apical dominance. Soon the lateral bud closest to the top will straighten up and become a new apex. In a short while it will take over apical dominance, and again any lateral growth will be inhibited.

6. If the new apical bud is cut off, too, the cycle starts all over again.

In short, if you cut off the top of a plant it will usually react by sending out branches. If you don't, it will do most of its growing straight up until it is pruned accidentally or naturally, as was my seasick lemon tree. Or until it begins to branch by a method so complicated and debatable I prefer to say "it just felt like branching."

For pruning most young after-dinner plants, a pair of large sharp household scissors is usually adequate. I understand I am *not* to use Susan's sewing shears, even if they are the largest and sharpest in the house. In the case of older woody plants beginning to grow bark, an adolescent mango or avocado, for instance, a pair of pruning shears may be needed. Whichever you use, make the cut as clean as possible, avoiding tearing or stripping the bark along the stem.

Cutting should be done at a slant, and relatively close but

not right down to a bud or leaf. Don't be afraid to cut back the apical bud considerably, and a branch entirely, if necessary. Except when trimming off a whole branch, however, always leave a bud or leaf just behind or below the bottom edge of each cut. If all the new and potential growth were to be removed at once, you'd end up with a brown beanpole. Ideal for growing vines on, but no longer a contributing member, in good green standing, of your jungle.

23

The Ungrateful Caterpillar and Sundry Such Intruders

A great number of visitors are naturally drawn to an after-dinner garden. Most of these are friends who have dropped by and who, on seeing the lush windows, inquire obliquely if you could spare a plant. Or, more directly, once they find out the jungle has sprouted from seed, how they, too, can manage an after-dinner plantation. But there are some more unexpected callers, whose presence at first might appear benign, but who change their roles the moment your back is turned. Such was the case with the malevolent caterpillar who dropped in one summer day and whom I let hang around for local color.

After all, I told myself, a little animal life for the jungle was just what it needed. An ocelot, which I privately would have preferred, was out of the question, at least so I gathered from Susan's response to discreet hints in that direction around my birthday. So I settled for Casper the caterpillar, and let him crawl his multifooted way. How he immigrated in the first place will always remain a mystery. The window was open, certainly, but we were on the fifth floor, and three sets of fire escape stairs with no bottom set seems a rather steep jump for a two-inch caterpillar.

Whatever Casper's itinerary, upon my return the evening after his arrival, I had cause to regret my hospitality. He, or maybe she or it, I'm not certain as to the proper mode of address here, was sitting on my prize mango, merrily munching on one of the youngest, greenest, and most delicious leaves. When I picked him, her, or it, up, he, she, or it promptly rolled into a ball and sulked.

"Tough," I remarked and put him, her, it firmly on the window ledge outside and closed the window behind it. Opening the window from the top, I left Casper to fend for himself.

A week later a caterpillar again peered at me from among the undergrowth of my jungle. Being unable to tell one caterpillar from the other, I could only assume it was the same tenacious hairy cat. This time I put him, her, it in a covered cup and took it down to the park. So much for caterpillars.

The next invasion, and this was really a storming of my windowsill citadel, occurred shortly after I planted the sugarcane. As an experiment, I had left one of the cuttings propped up in the soil without a top hat of wax. The next day, hopefully checking the bud for any swelling indicative of intentions to sprout, I couldn't help but notice the lively brown ribbon weaving its way from my coconut to my sugarcane pot. The top of the cane resembled a shopping center parking lot the day before Christmas. Ants. Hundreds of ants. The coconut husk, before moving to our apartment, it would seem, had been a regular, if diminutive, housing development. Now they wanted to move out to suburbia. Closer inspection of the rest of my jungle setting showed that an avocado pit had become a nursery for the habitat: several hundred larvae nestled beneath the soil on the shady side. Following the route of the scouts, I observed another colony of the settlers on the litchi pot. Enough was enough. Besides, the tiny beasts bit. Two little ant traps at the crossroads between the most savory plants took care of the lot of them in a week.

Insects are not the only unexpected guests that might decide to stay and take up residence in an after-dinner garden. For a while three diminutive maples grew next to my pineapple pot.

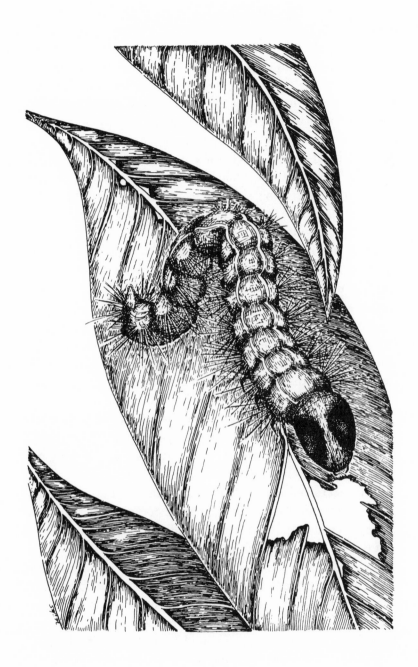

They were almost more of a mystery than Casper, since as far as I could ascertain the nearest maple was about three blocks away.

At least the maples had the horticultural advantage that I could identify them. Another, somewhat droopy and out-of-place-looking tree once took up residence in an abandoned coffee can. I had no idea of what it was or where it came from. It sprouted unexpectedly among the toothpicks labeled GRAPE-VINES, the latter long since transplanted to terra-cotta. No doubt it also made its way out of the everywhere through the open summer window.

Most visitors are not too persistent in their house calls. The previously mentioned invasions occurred over a period of three years. But there are some more frequent and considerably less inviting customers. One of these is the plant louse, or aphid. Where it materializes from in the hustle and bustle of city life is a question I can't answer. But the aphids arrive in the late spring with fair regularity. Their advent is no occasion to be softhearted. Individually so small (usually about a sixteenth of an inch long) as to go unnoticed, collectively they are a destructive menace. And there's no waiting in line to get in. They'll sit three deep if they have to, in a particularly juicy niche. Cases have been recorded of heavily infested farms being destroyed by them in a matter of a week or less.

It doesn't even take two to tango. Many aphids reproduce parthenogenetically, that is, the female doesn't bother with the male, but just keeps on reproducing all by herself. And I found out that, while the life of the average aphid is short, only three to five weeks, it crams a lot into that brief time. Each female gives birth to three to seven young aphids a day for about three weeks running. Her little aphids will in turn start their own families within a few days. I've even heard of cases where aphids were born pregnant. Now the way I see it, if one aphid flies in the window, there are five or six the next day and a

dozen or so around the day after that. The third day there are almost twenty offspring from the original aphid. The six first-born proceed then and there to have thirty-six or so offspring among them, which added to the rest of the family gives a count of fifty-six. The fourth day twenty-five birth announcements from the firstborn aphids, seventy-two from the second generation, and about two hundred from the third generation put the total at well over three hundred.

With an aphid collection keeping up that pace, by the end of a week we'd have several thousand of them around. By the second week Susan had better find a recipe for aphid soup, or we'd be in trouble.

Luckily a ladybug landed shortly after my first aphid invasion. Ladybugs love aphids best, for breakfast, lunch, and dinner. She made short work of a great many aphids. Unfortunately, by then the tenth generation was well on its way, and the gracious ladybug, having seemingly developed ulcers, departed wordlessly.

But her visit gave me time to work out alternative solutions to the aphid disposal problem. If you can't count on a ladybug with an appetite dropping in to dine, other remedies include a number of available sprays containing malathion or rotenone. I myself will avoid malathion wherever I can, because it is particularly odiferous and dangerous; and the other sprays seem just as effective, so I use them if I must use one at all. An emergency aphid crisis can be dealt with by almost any of the sprays made for the job available at the local garden department. But all pesticide sprays should be used carefully and sparingly; they can be fatal to you as well as to aphids.

By far the better solution, if you can spot the frolicking aphids before geometric progression sets in, is to simply wash them away. Placing the plant in a basin and spraying each leaf, and particularly the joint where it is attached to the branch, thoroughly with lukewarm water from a flower bulb, also available at the local discount store, usually does the trick. The plain water bath has much to recommend it, not the least of which is safety, particularly when there are children around, since chemical sprays, innocently misused, can be fatal.

The one visitor that never tapped on my windowpane was the one I'd been waiting for all along. A bee or two. Of course bees have a nose for flowers, and even in summer, with all the windows open, there's not so very much to lure them to the green foliage of an indoor jungle. Then again, I'm not certain there are any in the city. I imagine bee survival would be rather hazardous among the glass and concrete high rises. But I intended to have bees all the same—even if I had to buy them and put up a hive on the balcony. In New York, as they say, you can get anything. And in downtown Manhattan there was in fact a bee merchant. Even if I wasn't a potential future bee farmer I was tempted to go down and buy some, just to see how he got several thousand bees to sit still long enough to be weighed—he sold them by the pound.

24

Thirty-one Rules—To Break If You Feel Like It

An indoor jungle is a personal thing. All the rules in the world may be no help at all in your special situation. The most important thing is to really want to grow the plants. I'm not saying they're emotional and will feel rejected if you don't treat them as part of the family. But it's only natural that they will be better cared for if you're interested in them. Some people find no sense of wonder in watching a carefully nurtured seed germinate and grow from a spindly stalk into a maturing plant, each leaf unfolding and developing in its own special way. All they want is something green in the corner, a decorative piece that goes well with the drapes and furniture arrangement. True, plants can do much to enhance a room, but if what they'd like is simply ornamentation, I'd recommend—even though personally I can't abide them—plastic plants. Once they're installed and bent to the most appropriate shape, you can forget about them.

A living tree, on the other hand, is going to be somewhat more demanding. It will sooner or later borrow most of your kitchen equipment, abscond with the lazy Susan, insist one day on a full-fledged fog in your living room that curls up the edges of the prints hung on the walls, hog all the best light in the house, send you out on a winter's day for vitamins, and demand that your floor be lowered. The coconut you thought would look so nice at the far right of the corner window will claim for itself the status of centerpiece on the dining room table—and please lower the chandelier—while it recuperates from a case of chills it got by the window. The grapevine won't let you open the window it's curled around.

Nevertheless, with some give-and-take a very happy coexistence can be achieved with a jungle. For the most part a plant will respond to any reasonable compromise offer in a particular clash of interests, human versus horticultural. And the reason rules aren't necessarily applicable is that sweeping statements of how things worked in one place one time, or even several times, don't guarantee that they will continue to work that way, or that there's no other way. Particularly if any of the circumstances are different. However, I found a few basic ground rules that make a workable plan for life in your own jungle.

Watering

1. Use tepid water for watering all your plants. They don't like cold baths any more than most of the rest of us do.

2. Water plants at dusk or even at night. Although it probably rains on this earth as often during the day as during the night, evening is when the dew falls. Besides, direct sun shining on newly watered leaves will often burn them.

3. It's better to water well twice a week than a little every day. Remember, more people overwater than underwater their plants.

4. Water plants from the bottom at least once every two weeks. Variety is the spice of life, even for roots.

5. Place your plant pots on a dish of pebbles. This will keep the bottom of the pot from standing in water. The wet pebbles also have a large surface area, so evaporation of water will be rapid, keeping the area around the plants high in humidity.

6. Tropical plants like a softly moist atmosphere. For that matter, it's healthier for you, too. Spray the leaves occasionally.

However, if the leaves curl around their edges afterward, your apartment is so dry that the water is evaporating too quickly to be natural. In that case, spray around the plant instead of directly into its leaves. Or move the plant to the bathroom; it's usually one of the most humid places in an apartment. The plants might not convert your bathtub to a tropical lagoon—then again they might.

7. Try double potting if your apartment is extremely dry and the bathroom is overgrown with jungle. Place a plant potted in a porous terra-cotta pot inside a larger, nonporous pot. Fill the space between the two pots with peat moss or sphagnum. Water both the soil and the moss. This will keep the humidity high. Of course a nice, uncovered aquarium near your plants will do just about the same job—and add a little animal life at the same time.

8. Water is not always water. If yours is heavily chlorinated, let it stand in an open container overnight before using. Don't use water that has been "softened"; the chemicals used in this process tend to collect in the pot, killing the plants.

Lighting

9. Plants are outdoor creatures and love the sun, but strong, prolonged sunlight is rarely good for a plant in its first weeks of growth. After all, outside it would usually spend its childhood in the shade of more mature plants.

10. Plants can spend their entire life under artificial light, so don't let lamp-lit corners go bare of greenery.

11. When transferring a plant from genuine light to artificial light, or vice versa, remember that the plant will be undergoing a slight case of shock and will probably lose a few of its older leaves. Don't fertilize for a week or two after moving. Let it recuperate. One change at a time is enough.

12. Under artificial light, particularly fluorescent, soil takes

on a slightly different color. It will often look as moist as the soil in your pots by the window, and yet be bone dry.

Soil and Fertilization

13. Dig up the surface soil in your pots with a fork every two or three weeks. Plants have to breathe, and soil that is constantly watered tends to pack. Just be careful of the roots, particularly when dealing with plants whose roots tend to be shallow.

14. Fertilize your plants carefully by the directions given with the particular plant food, whether liquid or in tablet form, that you're using. Don't overfertilize. But, just as important, don't forget to fertilize. Plants have to eat, too.

15. Try to avoid using the same plant food all the time. Fertilizer ingredients vary, and a different kind might have a trace of just what's needed for an occasional boost. Besides, how would you like to eat spaghetti every day of your life?

16. If you ever have cigar-smoking company, bring one of the potted plants over for use as an ashtray. Tobacco itself is bad for the plant, so restrain your guest from putting the butt out in the soil. But let him flick the ash into the pot as often as he likes. Cigar or cigarette ash is very high in potassium, which helps make the leaves green.

17. The Pilgrims learned from Native Americans to stick a fish in with the corn kernels they planted. As the fish decayed it provided a rich fertilizer for the growing plant. I haven't donated any sardines yet. But another perfectly good after-dinner fertilizer is eggshells. Don't use the whole shell, just the inner membrane. Let the eggshells soak in water overnight, then fish them out and use the water on the plants. They'll lap it up.

18. Plants have to take a break, too. All plants have a dormant period. This is usually shorter for tropical plants than for

their temperate-zone cousins. But short or long, the time will come when they just sit there. Let them sit. Water as usual, but don't fertilize. A little sleep never hurt anyone. After a month or so, when you see new buds on a waking plant, give it a good fertilizer breakfast.

19. Soil texture is almost as important as fertilization. Old soil tends to "feel funny," not at all crumbly and good the way soil should. When a potted plant has remained in the same pot for two to three years, it needs some fresh soil. Turn the pot upside down, if it isn't too big and heavy, and keep tapping it until the plant loosens and falls out. Needless to say, you have to hold one hand spread across the pot, plant between your fingers, when you do this. If you can't tap it out, lay the thing on its side, get a hammer and break the pot. You can always cover the hole in the new pot with the shattered pieces of this one. Scratch out the loose soil between the exterior roots with a pencil, but be delicate so as not to injure the roots. Removing as much as you can of the old soil leaves more room for the fresh stuff.

First Aid

20. If a plant's leaves begin to turn brown at the tips, chances are you're either overwatering or overfertilizing the plant.

21. If the leaves curl and brown, and you're not overwatering, chances are it's too warm or the air is too dry.

22. If the leaves turn pale or yellow, check the roots. If they wind around most of the space afforded by the pot, it's time to transplant to bigger quarters. If the roots are not pot-bound, try giving the plant more fertilizer, particularly iron. If, on the other hand, the roots look or smell rotten, you're overwatering.

23. If leaves drop off when they're not supposed to, the plant is probably suffering from too little humidity or fertilizer. Or it's gotten into a cold draft.

24. "Cotton" on a plant you're sure isn't a cotton bush, particularly prevalent on avocados, is caused by the mealy bug. Wash off the white with rubbing alcohol, using a cotton swab. Keep it up until cotton is no longer king. But try to limit the alcohol rub to only infested areas.

25. If a plant just seems in general to be struggling for survival, give it a new home, even if you just transplant it, with fresh soil, to a pot the same size. Everyone likes their mattress turned occasionally.

Sundry

26. Keep several potted plants next to each other. For tropical plants this is a particularly good idea, since in that fashion they form a "minijungle" with an appropriately higher humidity.

27. Clean plant leaves occasionally, using moist cheesecloth. City soot clogs up the leaves' breathing pores. So does oil; don't use it to try to get the leaves glossier than nature. Better than damp-dusting, give the plants an occasional good shower. The bathtub is an excellent place for this. Don't use the showerhead; that's too hard a pelting for most plants. Use a regular spray bulb found at any garden center. But the bathtub saves worrying where the excess water is going.

28. Fuzzy leaves, like those of the Chinese gooseberry, shouldn't be cleaned with water at all. They retain the water and tend to develop brown spots. Use a soft brush, like a watercolor brush, to remove the dust and grime.

29. Avoid drafts. You might only get a stiff neck from them, but plants will die.

For vacation plans, you can count on most healthy plants weathering a week without water easily. If you are going away for a longer period, or have some plants that are very watery-stemmed, consequently wilting more readily, cover them with a plastic bag from the dry cleaner's. Prop four chopsticks, or

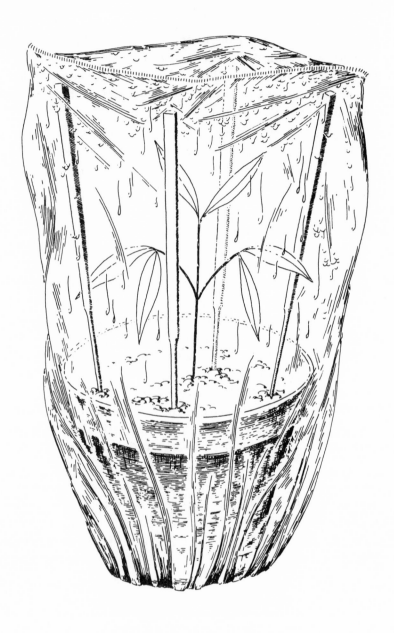

bamboo slats if the plant is tall, in the pot and tent the plastic over the whole affair, tucking it under the pot around the bottom. This will keep a plant thriving for as long as three weeks. But don't keep bagged plants where they will be reached by more than an hour of direct sun a day, or you'll have boiled greens when you come back.

31. Move your plants around once in a while. Everyone likes a change of scene. Also, moved to a different setting, an old familiar plant you've been absently staring past the last few months catches your eye and looks quite like a new and different creature.

Last, but certainly not least, as they say, I learned to experiment. Nature has made people look foolish so often, there was no honest reason I should try to avoid my quota of horticultural chagrin. Any new fruit or vegetable we found I'd try to coax to sprout, and I soon lost any shyness I'd originally had about varying the conditions under which my plants grew if one set didn't work to my satisfaction. Granted, I lost plants this way occasionally, but that's the breaks of the game.

For certain very stubborn cases of nongermination, lately I've even been contemplating modifying a method I once read about. Some time ago the *Wall Street Journal* reported that "Florida fruit growers are planning to waft music into their mango groves in hopes of producing bigger, tastier fruit." That seemed to offer a whole new approach to things. Perhaps I'll try for a Mozart Mango.

Further Reading for
the Intrepid After-Dinner Gardener

The following is a list of some of the more interesting volumes I've found in my botanical wanderings. Not all of them are in print, but they can usually be found in libraries. If you can't find a particular title, don't fret. Almost every book you do read will refer you to others, in an endless chain, towards the end of which is one, *Botanico-Periodicum-Huntianum*, which in 1,100 pages does nothing but list magazines for further reading. Squinting at the title and applying my imagination, I could even read it as "Botanical-Periodical-Hunting Guide."

Bailey, L. H. *Manual of Cultivated Plants*, rev. ed. New York: Macmillan, 1949.

———. *The Standard Cyclopedia of Horticulture*. Three vols. New York: Macmillan, 1943.

Barrett, O. W. *The Tropical Crops*. New York: Macmillan, 1928.

Batchelor, L. D., and H. J. Webber, eds. *The Citrus Industry*. Two vols. Berkeley: University of California Press, 1948.

Canham, A. E. *Artificial Light in Horticulture*. Eindhoven, Netherlands: Centrex, 1966.

Chandler, W. H. *Evergreen Orchards*. Philadelphia: Lea & Febiger, 1950.

Childers, N. F. *Mineral Nutrition of Fruit Crops*. New Brunswick: Rutgers University Horticultural Publications, 1954.

Coit, J. E. *Citrus Fruits*. New York: Macmillan, 1917.

Collins, J. L. *The Pineapple: Botany, Cultivation and Utilization*. New York: Interscience, 1960.

Cooper, W. C. *In Search of the Golden Apple.* New York: Vantage Press, 1982.

Copeland, E. B. *The Coconut.* London: Macmillan, 1931.

Deerr, N. *The History of Sugar.* Two vols. London: Chapman & Hall, 1949.

Devlin, R. M. *Plant Physiology.* New York: Reinhold, 1966.

Earle, F. S. *Sugarcane and Its Culture.* New York: John Wiley & Sons, 1928.

Fairchild, D. *The World Was My Garden.* New York: Charles Scribner's Sons, 1938.

Fawcett, W. *The Banana, Its Cultivation, Distribution and Commercial Uses,* 2nd ed. London: Duckworth & Co., 1921.

Firminger, T. A. C. *Manual of Gardening for Bengal and Upper India.* London: R. C. Lepage & Co., 1888.

Gangolly, S. R., R. Singh, and D. Singh. *The Mango.* New Delhi: Council of Agricultural Research, 1957.

Gerth van Wijk, H. L. *A Dictionary of Plant Names.* Two vols. The Hague: Martinus Nijhoff, 1911.

Getchell, A. A. *Sugar Cane Physiology.* New York: Elsevier Scientific Pub., 1973.

Groff, G. W. *The Lychee and Lungan.* New York: Orange Judd Co., 1921.

Hill, A. F. *Economic Botany: A Textbook of Useful Plants and Plant Products.* New York: McGraw-Hill, 1952.

Hine, R. B., O. V. Holtzmann, and R. D. Raabe. *Diseases of Papaya in Hawaii.* Hawaii Agricultural Experiment Station Bulletin 136 (July 1965).

Hodgson, R. W. *The Pomegranate.* California Agricultural Experiment Station Bulletin 276: 163–192 (Jan. 1917).

Hume, H. H. *Citrus Fruits.* New York: Macmillan, 1957.

Joubert, A. J. "The Litchi." *Pretoria Agricultural Technical Services Bulletin 389* (1970).

Lim, T. K., and K. K. Chong. *Diseases and Disorders of Mango in Malaysia.* Kuala Lumpur: Tropical Press, 1985.

von Loesecke, H. W. *Bananas.* New York: Interscience, 1950.

Menon, K. P. V., and K. M. Pandalai. *The Coconut Palm.* Ernakulam, S. India: Indian Central Coconut Committee, 1958.

Morton, J. F. *Fruits of Warm Climates.* Winterville, NC: Creative Resource Systems, 1987.

Ochse, J. J., M. J. Soule, Jr., M. J. Dijkman, and C. Wehlburg. *Tropical and Subtropical Agriculture.* New York: Macmillan, 1961.

Popenoe, P. B. *Date Growing in the Old World and the New.* Altadena, CA: West India Gardens, 1913.

Popenoe, W. *Manual of Tropical and Subtropical Fruits.* New York: Macmillan, 1924.

Py, C., J-J. Lacoeulhe, and C. Teisson. *The Pineapple.* Paris: G. P. Maisonneuve & Larose, 1987.

Reynolds, P. K. *The Banana: Its History, Cultivation and Place among Staple Foods.* Boston: Houghton Mifflin, 1927.

Shigeura, G. T., and R. M. Bullock. *The Guava in Hawaii.* Honolulu: University of Hawaii at Manoa, 1983.

Shurtleff, M. C. *How to Control Plant Diseases in Home and Garden.* Ames: Iowa State University Press, 1966.

Simmonds, N. W. *Bananas.* London: Longmans, Green & Co. Ltd., 1959.

———. *The Evolution of the Bananas.* New York: John Wiley & Sons, 1962.

Singh, L. B. *The Mango: Botany, Cultivation and Utilization.* New York: Interscience, 1960.

Steward, F. C. *About Plants: Topics in Plant Biology.* Reading, MA: Addison-Wesley, 1966.

Storey, W. B. *The Fig: Ficus carica Linnaeus.* Riverside, CA: Jurupa Mountains Cultural Center, 1977.

U.S. Department of Agriculture. *Growing the Jerusalem Artichoke.* No. 116 (June 1936).

Yee, W., and G. Aoki. *Papaya Culture in Hawaii.* Preliminary Circular (April 1965). Hawaii: College of Tropical Agriculture, University of Hawaii.